Production Sets

This is a volume in
ECONOMIC THEORY, ECONOMETRICS, AND MATHEMATICAL
 ECONOMICS

A Series of Monographs and Textbooks

Consulting Editor: KARL SHELL

A complete list of titles in this series appears at the end of this volume.

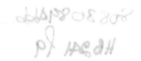

Production Sets

Edited by *MURRAY C. KEMP*

SCHOOL OF ECONOMICS
UNIVERSITY OF NEW SOUTH WALES
KENSINGTON, NEW SOUTH WALES
AUSTRALIA

1982

ACADEMIC PRESS
A Subsidiary of Harcourt Brace Jovanovich, Publishers

New York   London
Paris   San Diego   San Francisco   São Paulo   Sydney   Tokyo   Toronto

ACADEMIC PRESS, INC.
111 Fifth Avenue, New York, New York 10003

United Kingdom Edition published by
ACADEMIC PRESS, INC. (LONDON) LTD.
24/28 Oval Road, London NW1 7DX

Library of Congress Cataloging in Publication Data
Main entry under title:

Production sets.

(Economic theory, econometrics, and mathematical
economics)
    Includes index.
    Contents: A Baedeker / Murray C. Kemp -- On the
flatness of the transformation surface / Murray C. Kemp,
Chulsoon Khang, and Yasuo Uekawa -- The properties of
the set of production possibilities with pure
intermediate products / Makoto Tawada -- The shape of the
world production frontier / Makoto Tawada -- [etc.]
    1. Production functions (Economic theory)--Addresses,
essays, lectures. I. Kemp, Murray C. II. Series.
HB241.P758 1982   338.5'01   82-13922
ISBN 0-12-404140-X

PRINTED IN THE UNITED STATES OF AMERICA

82 83 84 85   9 8 7 6 5 4 3 2 1

Contents

11 Exhaustible resources and the set of feasible present-value production points

MURRAY C. KEMP AND MAKOTO TAWADA

12 Some properties of the per capita production set in the two-sector model of economic growth

NGO VAN LONG

List of Contributors

Numbers in parentheses indicate the pages on which the authors' contributions begin.

HORST HERBERG (69, 89), Institut für Theoretische Volkswirtschaftslehre, Christian-Albrechts-Universität zu Kiel, 23 Kiel 1, West Germany

MURRAY C. KEMP (1, 11, 39, 69, 89, 135), School of Economics, University of New South Wales, Kensington, New South Wales 2033, Australia

CHULSOON KHANG (11), Department of Economics, University of Oregon, Eugene, Oregon 97403

NGO VAN LONG (145), Department of Economics, School of General Studies, Australian National University, Canberra 2600, Australia

RICHARD MANNING (39, 51, 119), Department of Economics, University of Canterbury, Christchurch 1, New Zealand

JOHN McMILLAN (119), Department of Economics, University of Western Ontario, London, Ontario, Canada N6A 5C2

KAZUO NISHIMURA (39), Department of Economics, Tokyo Metropolitan University, Tokyo, Japan

MAKOTO TAWADA (17, 25, 39, 89, 109, 135), Department of Economics, Kobe University of Commerce, Tarumi, Kobe, Japan 655

YASUO UEKAWA (11), Department of Economics, Kobe University of Commerce, Tarumi, Kobe, Japan 655

Preface

In the theory of production sets one easily discerns two disjoint traditions that long have stood in a relationship of amicable indifference to each other. In the older tradition, stretching back to Torrens and Ricardo and reaching a high point with the editing by Tjalling Koopmans of the conference proceedings *Activity Analysis of Production and Allocation* (1951), the set of production possibilities available to a community is derived from knowledge of (i) the available quantities of primary (unproduced) factors of production and of (ii) a finite set of constant-returns activities (the book of blueprints). In the younger tradition, the book of blueprints is replaced by a finite set of production functions, each of which admits smooth substitutions of factors and products.

Within the older tradition, the properties of production sets have been very thoroughly worked out. Koopman's *Activity Analysis* remains by far the most authoritative and complete statement. In contrast, published analysis of production sets within the younger tradition has been fragmentary and unsystematic. Makoto Tawada's doctoral thesis, *The Properties of the Set of Production Possibilities* (University of New South Wales, 1980), does provide a thorough treatment of several fundamental issues but remains unpublished.

The essays collected here are all in the second or younger tradition. Between them they provide a quite comprehensive account of the properties of production sets. All were written within the past few years, nearly all of them by individuals with a regular or transient association with the University of New South Wales.

Most of the chapters are published here for the first time. Chapters 2, 5, and 7–9 are exceptions. Chapter 2 first appeared in the *Journal of International Economics* of November 1978, Chapter 5 in the *Journal of International Economics* of August 1980, Chapter 7 in the *Canadian Journal of Economics* of August 1969, Chapter 8 in the *Journal of International Economics* of August 1982, and Chapter 9 in *Econometrica* of May 1980. To the proprietors of those journals, North-Holland Publishing Company, Amsterdam (Chapters 2, 5, and 8), the Econometric Society (Chapter 9), and the Canadian Economics Association (Chapter 7), I am grateful for permission to reprint.

A Baedeker

MURRAY C. KEMP

In this introduction I provide a brief history of the analysis of sets of production possibilities (production sets), hoping thereby to define the gaps that the remaining chapters are intended to fill.

1. THE PRODUCTION SET OF A SINGLE COUNTRY—NONJOINT PRODUCTION

The concept of the production set of a single country is central to nearly all branches of modern macroeconomic theory. However, the concept has not always played so prominent a role. Until after World War II only trade theorists made any substantial use of it; and for well over a century, beginning with the expositions of Torrens and Ricardo, the theory of international trade was dominated by the assumption that there is a single factor of production that produces nonjointly under conditions of constant returns. Needless to say, under that assumption the properties of the production set are transparent: the upper boundary of the set (the transformation locus) is a simple hyperplane. Only with the abandonment of the assumption could a nontrivial theory of production sets emerge.

Nonlinear transformation loci, in two dimensions, made their appearance in the late twenties and early thirties—one recalls, in particular, the contributions of Young (1928), Haberler (1930), Lerner (1932), Leontief (1933), and Viner (1937). The early drawings were rather impressionistic; however, justification of the now conventional bowed-out shape was provided, eventually, in the second (1949) of Samuelson's two papers on factor-price equalization in two-by-two or Heckscher–Ohlin models of production.

At this stage (1949) no one had tackled the general or $m \times n$ case. However, with the publication of Koopmans (1951), the profession became acquainted with the approach to production theory through linear activity analysis and, in particular, learned that, if there is just a finite number of activities, whether or not there is joint production, then the production transformation locus is concave and composed of flats or linear facets.

The properties of the production set when factors and products can be smoothly substituted for each other remained unknown. Indeed, the systematic examination of those properties did not begin until the late sixties. During the intervening period we have only Samuelson's (1953) remark that when products outnumber factors, the transformation surface necessarily contains flat segments, a remark that was later verified in the context of 3×2 models of Kemp and Jones (1962) and Melvin (1968). However, during the past 15 years there has been a sustained attempt to unravel the properties of production sets under quite general conditions. The ball was set rolling by Quirk and Saposnik (1966), who demonstrated that if production is nonjoint and if production functions are homogeneous of degree one and quasi-concave, then the production set of a single country is convex (see also Herberg and Kemp, 1969; Herberg, 1973). The next step was taken by Khang (1971) and Khang and Uekawa (1973), who, under the same general assumptions, established necessary and sufficient conditions for the transformation locus of a single country to be strictly concave. Then, terminating that particular line of thought, at least for the time being, Kemp *et al.* (1978) provided necessary and sufficient conditions for the appearance in the transformation surface of a single country of flats of any dimension. That paper appears as Chapter 2 in the present volume. In Chapter 3, Tawada treats in detail a special case of interest to trade and public-finance theorists.

2. THE WORLD PRODUCTION SET

The concept of a production set first found favor among theorists of international trade. It is not surprising, therefore, that they soon extended the notion to accommodate the entire trading world. Thus, barely 2 years after the appearance of Haberler's paper (1930), Lerner (1932), confining himself to the two-goods case, showed how to derive the world production set from the sets of particular countries. He showed that if each single-country transformation curve is strictly concave and if all factors are internationally quite immobile, then the world transformation curve also is strictly concave.

If we turn a blind eye to McKenzie's (1954) work, which embraced any number of commodities but only one factor, matters remained where Lerner left them until the late sixties. Then, in a series of papers, Kemp (1966), Jones (1967), Inada and Kemp (1969), Chipman (1971), and Uekawa (1972) marginally extended the 2×2 Heckscher–Ohlin model of world production by allowing for the possibility that one factor of production is internationally mobile. In particular, it was shown by Chipman and Uekawa that the world production transformation curve may contain a line segment even though each single-country transformation curve is strictly concave.

There remained the difficult task of describing the properties of production sets in the general case in which countries, factors, and products are arbitrary in number and in which some of the factors and products are internationally mobile, others immobile. In Chapter 4, Tawada provides the required description and, in particular, derives necessary and sufficient conditions for the world production transformation surface to contain flats of any dimension. The earlier results of Lerner, McKenzie, Chipman, and Uekawa fall into place as special cases.

3. JOINT PRODUCTION

It is noteworthy that, in nearly all recent work on production sets with smooth substitutability of factors, production is taken to be nonjoint. The work of Herberg (1973) and Otani (1973) is an exception. Herberg and Otani provided a systematic examination of the convexity, closedness, and boundedness of production sets under assumptions that admit jointness. However, they confined themselves to sufficient conditions; moreover, they put aside questions relating to the degree of flatness in the production transformation surface. Recently, a comprehensive treatment of single-country and world production sets under quite general assumptions has been provided by Kemp *et al.*

(1980). Their paper is here reproduced as Chapter 5. And in Chapter 6 Manning develops a local but otherwise very general nonsubstitution theorem for joint-production technologies.

4.   VARIABLE RETURNS TO SCALE

All of the work reported in Sections 2 and 3 has been based on the assumption of constant returns to scale. The assumption is convenient but highly special. It is not surprising, therefore, that in recent years there have been several attempts to do away with it. Among the earliest of these we recall Herberg (1969), Kemp (1969), and Herberg and Kemp (1969, 1975). [I disregard those, like Tinbergen (1945, 1954), Matthews (1950), and Meade (1952), who drew production transformation curves for the case of variable returns but made little or no attempt to justify the shapes drawn.] Most notably, Herberg and Kemp showed that if industrial production functions are homothetic, then, roughly, near zero output of the jth good the curvature of the transformation surface in the (ij)-direction is determined by the nature of returns to scale in the jth industry only; in particular, the surface is conventionally concave if returns are decreasing and unconventionally convex if returns are increasing. They showed also that, away from the axes, the curvature of the surface depends not only on returns to scale but also on rates of change of returns to scale. With the addition of an appendix that rebuts the criticisms of Wolfgang Mayer (1974), the Herberg–Kemp paper is here reprinted as Chapter 7.

More recently, the results obtained by Herberg and Kemp have been extended by Herberg *et al.* (1982), who, in particular, allowed for the possibility that industries might generate externalities of production with incidence anywhere in the economy. That paper is here reprinted as Chapter 8.

5.   PUBLIC INTERMEDIATE GOODS

A new line of enquiry has been initiated recently by Manning and McMillan (1979) and by Tawada (1980a,b). Their contribution has been to allow for the possibility of public intermediate goods, like transport and communication networks and information in all of its many forms.

Two polar cases may be distinguished. In the first case, studied by Tawada, the individual industrial production functions are taken to be homogeneous of degree one in all inputs, public as well as private. Now the very publicness of public intermediate goods might have been thought to imbed in production processes an element of increasing returns and, in view of the work of Herberg and Kemp (1969), to destroy the convexity of the production set. Tawada's finding that the production transformation locus is necessarily strictly concave, however many primary factors, final goods, and public intermediate inputs, therefore came as a considerable surprise. Tawada's paper (1980a) is here reprinted as Chapter 9.

In the second case, studied by Manning and McMillan, the industrial production functions are taken to be homogeneous of degree one in primary factor inputs alone. On the basis of that assumption, Manning and McMillan were able to show that if there is a single primary factor, a single public intermediate good, and two final goods, then the production transformation locus is necessarily convex. Tawada (1980b) later showed that the conclusion remains valid for any number of final goods and any number of public intermediate goods but collapses when there are more than two primary factors.

The discoveries of Manning, McMillan, and Tawada left many unresolved but tantalizing questions. In particular, they left unexplored the entire middle ground between the two poles. What seems to be needed is a model of public intermediate goods sufficiently general to embrace both polar cases and such that one might discern those elements that generate convexity and those that generate nonconvexity. In Chapter 10, Manning and McMillan provide such a model.

6. EXHAUSTIBLE RESOURCES

In all studies of production sets known to me it has been assumed that primary factors of production cannot be exhausted or run down. How production sets might be defined in a context of exhaustibility has not been considered. The definitional problem is particularly acute if the resources are not only exhaustible but also nonreproducible and essential to production. For then there is the possibility that a nontrivial steady state may not exist. In Chapter 11 it is shown that this difficulty can be mastered by working with the notion of a set of vectors of present values of output streams.

7. THE 2 × 2 MODEL OF PRODUCTION

Throughout Chapters 2–11 the analysis accommodates any number of products and any number of factors. The emphasis is on generality, not pedagogy. In Chapter 12, by contrast, Long reexamines the familiar 2 × 2, or Heckscher–Ohlin, model of production. In particular, he derives the properties of the per capita production set (relating the two outputs to capital, all on a per capita basis) and then shows how those properties may be used to elucidate and integrate apparently quite disparate branches of economic theory—descriptive and optimal growth theory—and the economies of exhaustible resources.

8. FINAL REMARKS

There is a considerable literature dealing with the properties of "production sets" under conditions of market "distortion" by non-competitive elements, by taxes and subsidies, and by inertia of one kind or another (see, for example, Herberg and Kemp, 1971; Herberg *et al.*, 1971; Brecher, 1974). However, such sets are not production sets in the sense of the present volume; their upper boundaries are realizable under some well-defined market conditions, but generally they do not consist of efficient production points. Moreover, many of the distortions considered in the literature are in essence transitional and therefore are out of place in discussion of steady states. [For the dynamic behavior of models with temporary distortions, see Herberg and Kemp (1972) and Kemp *et al.* (1977).] For both reasons it has seemed appropriate to exclude such pseudoproduction sets from our consideration.

There is a smaller literature dealing with the properties of production sets when the supplies of primary factors of production respond to prices (see, for example, Walsh, 1956; Vanek, 1959; Kemp and Jones, 1962; Kemp, 1964). But these sets also are not production sets in our sense. For if the amount of a factor offered to the market varies with prices, then the factor must have an alternative nonmarket use (one thinks of parklands); and of the alternative product no notice is taken. Thus such sets are merely sections of production sets as we know them and are, from our point of view, of no special interest.

REFERENCES

Brecher, R. A. (1974). Minimum wage rates and the pure theory of international trade. *Quarterly Journal of Economics* **88**, 98–116.

Chipman, J. S. (1971). International trade with capital mobility: A substitution theorem. *In* "Trade, Balance of Payments, and Growth" (J. N. Bhagwati, R. W. Jones, R. A. Mundell, and J. Vanek, eds.), pp. 201–237. North-Holland Publ., Amsterdam.

Haberler, G. (1930). Die Theorie der komparativen Kosten. *Weltwirtschaftliches Archiv* **32**, 356–360.

Herberg, H. (1969). On the shape of the transformation curve in the case of homogeneous production functions. *Zeitschrift für die gesamte Staatswissenschaft* **125**, 202–210.

Herberg, H. (1973). On the convexity of the production possibility set under general production conditions. *Zeitschrift für die gesamte Staatswissenschaft* **129**, 205–214.

Herberg, H., and Kemp, M. C. (1969). Some implications of variable returns to scale. *Canadian Journal of Economics* **2**, 403–415 (reprinted as Chapter 7 in this volume).

Herberg, H., and Kemp, M. C. (1971). Factor market distortions, the shape of the locus of competitive outputs, and the relation between product price and equilibrium outputs. *In* "Trade, Balance of Payments, and Growth" (J. N. Bhagwati, R. W. Jones, R. A. Mundell, and J. Vanek, eds.), pp. 22–48. North-Holland Publ., Amsterdam.

Herberg, H., and Kemp, M. C. (1972). Growth and factor market "imperfections." *Zeitschrift für die gesamte Staatswissenschaft* **128**, 590–604.

Herberg, H., and Kemp, M. C. (1975). Homothetic production functions and the shape of the production possibility locus. *Journal of Economic Theory* **11**, 287–288.

Herberg, H., Kemp, M. C., and Magee, S. (1971). Factor market distortions, the relation between product prices and equilibrium outputs. *Economic Record* **47**, 518–530.

Herberg, H., Kemp, M. C., and Tawada, M. (1982). Further implications of variable returns to scale. *Journal of International Economics* **11**, in press (reprinted as Chapter 8 in this volume).

Inada, K., and Kemp, M. C. (1969). International capital movements and the theory of tariffs and trade: Comment. *Quarterly Journal of Economics* **83**, 524–528.

Jones, R. W. (1967). International capital movements and the theory of tariffs and trade. *Quarterly Journal of Economics* **81**, 1–38.

Kemp, M. C. (1964). "The Pure Theory of International Trade." Prentice-Hall, Englewood Cliffs, New Jersey.

Kemp, M. C. (1966). The gain from international trade and investment: A neo-Heckscher–Ohlin approach. *American Economic Review* **56**, 788–799.

Kemp, M. C. (1969). "The Pure Theory of International Trade and Investment." Prentice-Hall, Englewood Cliffs, New Jersey.

Kemp, M. C., and Jones, R. W. (1962). Variable labour supply and the theory of international trade. *Journal of Political Economy* **70**, 30–36.

Kemp, M. C., Kimura, Y., and Okuguchi, K. (1977). Monotonicity properties of a dynamic version of the Heckscher–Ohlin model of production. *Economic Studies Quarterly* **28**, 249–253.

Kemp, M. C., Khang, C., and Uekawa, Y. (1978). On the flatness of the transformation surface. *Journal of International Economics* **8**, 537–542 (reprinted as Chapter 2 in this volume).

Kemp, M. C., Manning, R., Nishimura, K., and Tawada, M. (1980). On the shape of the single-country and world commodity-substitution and factor-substitution surfaces under conditions of joint production. *Journal of International Economics* **10**, 395–404 (reprinted as Chapter 5 in this volume).

Khang, C. (1971). On the strict convexity of the transformation surface in case of linear homogeneous production functions: a general case. *Econometrica* **39**, 587–589.

Khang, C., and Uekawa, Y. (1973). The production possibility set in a model allowing interindustry flows: The necessary and sufficient conditions for its strict convexity. *Journal of International Economics* **3**, 283–290.

Koopmans, T. C., ed. (1951). "Activity Analysis of Production and Allocation." Wiley, New York.

Leontief, W. W. (1933). The use of indifference curves in the analysis of foreign trade. *Quarterly Journal of Economics* **47**, 493–503.

Lerner, A. P. (1932). The diagrammatical representation of cost conditions in international trade. *Economica* **12**, 346–356.

McKenzie, L. W. (1954). Specialization and efficiency in world production. *Review of Economic Studies* **21**, 165–180.

Manning, R., and McMillan, J. (1979). Public intermediate goods, production possibilities and international trade. *Canadian Journal of Economics* **12**, 243–257.

Matthews, R. C. O. (1950). Reciprocal demand and increasing returns. *Review of Economic Studies* **17**, 149–158.

Mayer, W. (1974). Variable returns to scale in general equilibrium theory: A comment. *International Economic Review* **15**, 225–235.

Meade, J. E. (1952). "A Geometry of International Trade." Allen & Unwin, London.

Melvin, J. R. (1968). Production and trade with two factors and three goods. *American Economic Review* **58**, 1249–1268.

Otani, Y. (1973). Neo-classical technology sets and properties of production possibility sets. *Econometrica* **41**, 667–682.

Quirk, J. P., and Saposnik, R. (1966). Homogeneous production functions and convexity of the production possibility set. *Metroeconomica* **18**, 192–197.

Samuelson, P. A. (1949). International factor price equalization once again. *Economic Journal* **59**, 181–197.

Samuelson, P. A. (1953). Prices of factors and goods in general equilibrium. *Review of Economic Studies* **21**, 1–20.

Tawada, M. (1980a). The production possibility set with public intermediate goods. *Econometrica* **47**, 1005–1010 (reprinted as Chapter 9 in this volume).

Tawada, M. (1980b). Properties of the set of production possibilities. Ph.D. thesis, University of New South Wales.

Tinbergen, J. (1945). "International Economic Cooperation." Elsevier, Amsterdam.

Tinbergen, J. (1954). "International Economic Integration." Elsevier, Amsterdam.

Uekawa, Y. (1972). On the existence of incomplete specialization in international trade with capital mobility. *Journal of International Economics* **2**, 1–23.

Vanek, J. (1959). An afterthought on the "real cost-opportunity cost" dispute and some aspects of general equilibrium under conditions of variable factor supplies. *Review of Economic Studies* 26, 198–208.

Viner, J. (1937). "Studies in the Theory of International Trade." Harper, New York.

Walsh, V. C. (1956). Leisure and international trade. *Economica, New Series* **23,** 253–260.
Young, A. A. (1928). Increasing returns and economic progress. *Economic Journal* **38,**
527–542.

SCHOOL OF ECONOMICS
UNIVERSITY OF NEW SOUTH WALES
KENSINGTON, NEW SOUTH WALES
AUSTRALIA

2

On the flatness of the transformation surface*

MURRAY C. KEMP

CHULSOON KHANG

YASUO UEKAWA

1. INTRODUCTION

Consider an economy equipped with any positive number of primary factors of production and any positive number of first-degree-homogeneous, concave, no-joint-products production functions, the inputs of which include produced commodities. It is known that for such an economy the locus of extreme net production possibilities (transformation surface) is concave to the origin. The locus is not necessarily strictly concave, a fact noted long ago by Samuelson (1953). However, Khang and Uekawa (1973) have provided necessary and sufficient conditions for strict concavity.

PROPOSITION 1: (Khang and Uekawa): Within the framework of the model, the transformation locus corresponding to "active" industries (in the sense that their gross outputs are positive) contains a linear segment if and only if the vectors of primary factors correspond-

* We are indebted to Michihiro Ohyama, Richard Manning, Makoto Tawada, and a referee for several penetrating comments. This chapter first appeared in *Journal of International Economics*, November 1978.

PRODUCTION SETS   ISBN 0-12-404140-X

ing to those active industries are linearly dependent (at the appropriate shadow prices of outputs).

This leaves unanswered the following question: Given that the locus is not strictly concave at some point, precisely what degree of flatness does it possess? In the present chapter we seek to answer that question. Our findings are summarized in Propositions 2 and 2' in Section 3.

2.   ASSUMPTIONS[1]

Let there be n produced commodities and m primary factors, $n \geqq m$. A produced commodity may be a pure consumption good, a pure intermediate good, or it may be both a final good and an intermediate good—such distinctions play no role in what follows. The nonnegative n-vector of gross outputs is denoted by $x \equiv (x_1, \ldots, x_n)$. The amounts of the jth good and kth primary factor employed in the ith industry are denoted by x_{ji} and v_{ki}, respectively. Thus the ith production function, defined on E_+^{n+m}, the nonnegative orthant of $(n + m)$-dimensional Euclidean space, is written as

$$x_i = f^i(z_i) \equiv f^i(x_{.i}, v_{.i})$$

where $x_{.i} \equiv (x_{1i}, \ldots, x_{ni})$ and $v_{.i} \equiv (v_{1i}, \ldots, v_{mi})$. The following restrictions are imposed on f^i.

(A1) f^i is continuous, homogeneous of degree one, and quasi-concave.

(A2)   *Either* (i) the economy is indecomposable, so that each proper subset of industries makes use of the output of at least one excluded industry, *or* (ii) each industry makes use of all primary factors.

The net output of the ith commodity is $y_i \equiv f^i - \sum_j x_{ij}$. If (as we suppose) all commodities are traded internationally, y_i may be of either sign. The net production set is

$$Y \equiv \{y \equiv (y_1, \ldots, y_n) \in E^n : y_i \leqq f^i(x_{.i}, v_{.i}) - \sum_j x_{ij} \text{ for}$$

$$\text{some } x_{.i} \geqq 0 \text{ and } v_{.i} \geqq 0, i = 1, \ldots, n, \text{ such}$$

$$\text{that } \sum_i v_{.i} \leqq v\}$$

[1] The notation is that of Khang and Uekawa (1973). The assumptions are somewhat weaker than those of Khang and Uekawa.

where $v \equiv (v_1, \ldots, v_m)$ is the constant vector of primary-factor endowments. The transformation surface is the upper boundary of Y.

3. ANALYSIS

Our task is to prove:

PROPOSITION 2:   Let $y*$ be a point in the transformation surface with n^0 industries active. Then the surface contains an $(n^0 - r)$-dimensional flat embracing $y*$ if and only if at $y*$ there are exactly r linearly independent vectors of primary-factor inputs.

Remark.   The plausibility of the proposition can be established by reflecting on the following familiar cases. (i) When $n = 2$ and $m = 1$ (the Torrens–Ricardo case) the transformation surface is a straight line in E^2, that is, the surface is a flat of dimension $n - r = n - m = 1$. (ii) When $n = 3$ and $m = 1$ the surface is a plane in E^3, that is, it is a flat of dimension $n - r = n - m = 2$. (iii) When $n = 3$ and $m = 2$, and when at no point in the surface do the three industries share a common ratio of primary factor inputs, then the surface is ruled or lined, that is, consists of flats of dimension $n - r = n - m = 1$ (see, for example, Kemp, 1964, Chapter 7; Melvin, 1968).

Proof.   (Sufficiency)   We have $y* = (y_1^*, \ldots, y_{n^0}^*; y_{n^0+1}^*, \ldots, y_n^*) \equiv (y_I^*, y_{II}^*)$, where $y_i^* = f^i(x_{\cdot i}^*, v_{\cdot i}^*) - \sum_{j=1}^{n^0} x_{ij}^*$ and $f^i(x_{\cdot i}^*, v_{\cdot i}^*)$ is positive for $1 \leq i \leq n^0$ and zero for $n^0 < i \leq n$. Let $V* \equiv (v_{\cdot 1}^{*T}, \ldots, v_{n^0}^{*T})$ have rank $r, r \leq \min(m, n^0)$, where T is the instruction to take the transpose. Now consider the system of homogeneous linear equations

$$ (1) \qquad\qquad\qquad V*c = 0 $$

The solution space in E^{n^0} is spanned by $n^0 - r$ independent vectors, say $c^1, \ldots, c^{n^0-r}$. Corresponding to any one of these vectors, say c^h (with ith component c_i^h), we may define the new input vectors

$$ (2) \quad z_i^h \equiv (x_{\cdot i}^h, v_{\cdot i}^h) \equiv (1 + \delta_h c_i^h)(x_{\cdot i}^*, v_{\cdot i}^*) \equiv (1 + \delta_h c_i^h)z_i^*, \qquad i = 1, \ldots, n^0 $$

where the scalar δ_h is so chosen that $1 + \delta_h c_i^h > 0$ and, therefore, $z_i^h \geq 0$. Corresponding to the new input vectors is the ith net output

$$ y_i^h = f^i(x_{\cdot i}^h, v_{\cdot i}^h) - \sum_{j=1}^{n^0} x_{ij}^h $$

$$ = (1 + \delta_h c_i^h)f^i(x_{\cdot i}^*, v_{\cdot i}^*) - \sum_{j=1}^{n^0} (1 + \delta_h c_j^h)x_{ij}^* $$

(Equation continues)

[from (2) and the homogeneity of f^i]

$$= f^i(x_{.i}^*, v_{.i}^*) - \sum_{j=1}^{n^0} x_{ij}^* + \delta_h c_i^h f^i(x_{.i}^*, v_{.i}^*) - \delta_h \sum_{j=1}^{n^0} c_j^h x_{ij}^*$$

$$= y_i^* + \delta_h(c_i^h x_i^* - \sum_{j=1}^{n^0} c_j^h x_{ij}^*)$$

In matrix notation,

(3) $y^h = y^* + \delta_h H^* c^h, \qquad H^* \equiv \begin{bmatrix} X^* - A_I^* \\ -A_{II}^* \end{bmatrix}$

where X^* is the diagonal matrix of order n^0 with x_i^* in the ith diagonal place, $i = 1, \ldots, n^0$, and

$$A_I^* \equiv \begin{bmatrix} x_{11}^* & \cdots & x_{1n^0}^* \\ \vdots & & \vdots \\ x_{n^0 1}^* & \cdots & x_{n^0 n^0}^* \end{bmatrix}, \qquad A_{II}^* \equiv \begin{bmatrix} x_{n^0+1,1}^* & \cdots & x_{n^0+1,n^0}^* \\ \vdots & & \vdots \\ x_{n1}^* & \cdots & x_{nn^0}^* \end{bmatrix}$$

We note that

$$\sum_{i=1}^{n^0} v_{.i}^h = \sum_{i=1}^{n^0} (1 + \delta_h c_i^h) v_{.i}^* = \sum_{i=1}^{n^0} v_{.i}^* + \delta_h \sum_{i=1}^{n^0} c_i^h v_{.i}^* \leqq v$$

implying that y^h is feasible.

Since the net production set is convex, there is associated with y^* a vector of shadow prices $p^* \equiv (p_I^*, p_{II}^*)$ such that $p_I^* > 0$ and

$$0 \geqq p^*(y^h - y^*) = \delta_h(p_I^*, p_{II}^*) H^* c^h$$

Since δ_h can be of either sign, $p^* y^h = p^* y^*$. Thus the line segment $\overline{y^* y^h}$ traced by δ_h, $1 + \delta_h c_i^h > 0$, lies in the transformation surface. Since h can take any of the values $1, \ldots, n^0 - r$, we have generated $n^0 - r$ such line segments.

We next show that these segments are linearly independent, or, equivalently, that the $n^0 - r$ vectors $(y^h - y^*)$ are linearly independent. From (3)

$$y^h - y^* = \delta_h \begin{bmatrix} X^* - A_I^* \\ -A_{II}^* \end{bmatrix} c^h, \qquad h = 1, \ldots, n^0 - r$$

that is, $y^h - y^*$ is a linear transformation of c^h. Now either (A2i) is satisfied, in which case $X^* - A_I^*$ is indecomposable and has a semi-dominant diagonal, or (A2ii) is satisfied, in which case $X^* - A_1^*$ has a dominant diagonal. In each case, $X^* - A_1^*$ has full rank. Moreover the c^h, $h = 1, \ldots, n^0 - r$, are linearly independent. Hence $y^h - y^*$, $h = 1, \ldots, n^0 - r$, are linearly independent.

To complete the proof of sufficiency we note that if the rank of V^* is r, then the dimension of the flat cannot exceed $n^0 - r$.[2]

(Necessity) Consider any point $y^* \equiv (y_1^*, y_{11}^*)$ in an $(n^0 - r)$-dimensional flat of the transformation surface. Let $V^* \equiv (v_{.1}^{*T}, \ldots, v_{.n^0}^{*T})$ be the matrix of primary-factor inputs to the n^0 active industries. Suppose that the rank of V^* is g, $g \neq r$. Then, from the sufficiency part of the proposition, the dimension of the flat must be $n^0 - g$, which is a contradiction. ∎

Remark. The substitution theorem of Samuelson (1951) is a special case of Proposition 2. Alternatively, one may view Proposition 2 as a generalization of the substitution theorem.[3]

Proposition 2 relates to a world with intermediate goods of the Leontief type but with no durable produced capital goods. However, it is possible to prove a proposition like Proposition 2 but relating to the locus of steady-state net-output vectors.

PROPOSITION 2': Consider an open economy with m primary factors each growing at the rate g, $g \geq 0$, and with n products each of which may be a consumption good and/or a perfectly durable capital good. Suppose that (A1) and (A2), suitably reinterpreted, are satisfied and that the own-rate of return to any capital good actually produced is equal to g. Let y^* be a point in the steady-state transformation surface, that is, the locus of steady-state net outputs (net after providing for the equipment of additional primary factors), with n^0 industries active. Then the surface contains an $(n^0 - r)$-dimensional flat embracing y^* if and only if at y^* there are exactly r linearly independent vectors of primary-factor inputs.

---

[2] From the proof of necessity in Khang and Uekawa (1973), we know that if there is a line segment (y', y'') in the transformation surface and passing through y^*, then there exists a unique nonzero vector c such that $y' - y^* = \hat{c}y^*$ and $Vc = 0$, where $\hat{c}$ is the diagonal matrix derived from c. It follows that the line segment $(y^*, y^* + \hat{c}y^*)$ defined by any vector c such that $Vc \neq 0$ is not in the surface.

[3] We note that there is a mistake in the proof of Corollary 3 of Khang and Uekawa (1973). In that proof an appeal is made to Corollary 1 of Khang and Uekawa (1973), but the appeal rests on the unwarranted assumption that if the transformation surface contains a nonlinear segment then it is convex.

Proof.   The proof is similar to that of Proposition 2.   ■

Remark.   One may view Proposition 2′ as a generalized "golden-age" substitution theorem.

Finally, we note that Proposition 2 can be extended to allow for the possibility of joint production and for the possibility that the number of production sectors differs from the number of final goods. One can then apply the result to that variant of the standard trade model in which one factor is internationally mobile, the other immobile. In that variant, there are four production sectors, two final goods, and three primary factors (one mobile, one immobile at home, and one immobile abroad).

REFERENCES

Kemp, M. C. (1964). "The Pure Theory of International Trade." Prentice-Hall, Englewood Cliffs, New Jersey.

Khang, C., and Uekawa, Y. (1973). The production possibility set in a model allowing interindustry flows: The necessary and sufficient conditions for its strict convexity. *Journal of International Economics* **3**, 283–290.

Melvin, J. R. (1968). Production and trade with two factors and three goods. *American Economic Review* **58**, 1249–1268.

Samuelson, P. A. (1951). Abstract of a theorem concerning substitutability in open Leontief models. *In* "Activity Analysis of Production and Allocation" (T. C. Koopmans, ed.), pp. 142–146. Wiley, New York.

Samuelson, P. A. (1953). Prices of factors and goods in general equilibrium. *Review of Economic Studies* **21**, 1–20.

Murray C. Kemp
SCHOOL OF ECONOMICS
UNIVERSITY OF NEW SOUTH WALES
KENSINGTON, NEW SOUTH WALES
AUSTRALIA

Chulsoon Khang
DEPARTMENT OF ECONOMICS
UNIVERSITY OF OREGON
EUGENE, OREGON

Yasuo Uekawa
DEPARTMENT OF ECONOMICS
KOBE UNIVERSITY OF COMMERCE
TARUMI, KOBE
JAPAN

3

The properties of the set of production possibilities with pure intermediate products*

MAKOTO TAWADA

1. INTRODUCTION

The shape of the production-possibility set crucially affects the theories of welfare economics and international trade. In particular, the convexity property of the production set plays an important role in the analysis of factor price equalization and in the proof of the Heckscher–Ohlin Theorem. Even if convexity is assured, there still remains another difficulty arising from the flatness of its frontier.

On the flatness of the production surface, Khang (1971) presented an elegant theorem. Since then, Khang and Uekawa (1973) and Kemp *et al.* (1978) extended Khang's result to accommodate interindustry flows. Tawada (1980) allowed for public intermediate goods and found that no flat can exist in the production frontier. Moreover, the case of joint production, which is another interesting problem, was studied by Kemp *et al.* (1980).

In the present chapter I consider in detail the special case in which there exists a category of pure intermediate goods. Such goods have figured prominently in the literature on "effective protection" and

* I wish to thank Professor M. C. Kemp for valuable comments and suggestions.

elsewhere.[1] In particular, I derive the necessary and sufficient conditions of any assigned degree of flatness in the production frontier. As a by-product, the nonsubstitutability of pure intermediate goods is shown.

2. THE MODEL AND THE ASSUMPTIONS

Consider an economy with n commodities, r intermediate goods, and m primary factors. Each commodity is produced by means of intermediate goods and primary factors, and each intermediate good is produced by means of primary factors. The production functions of the final commodities and intermediate goods are, respectively,

$$(1) \qquad\qquad X_i = F^i(V^i, M^i), \qquad i = 1, \ldots, n$$

and

$$(2) \qquad\qquad M_k = G^k(U^k), \qquad k = 1, \ldots, r$$

where $V^i = (V_1^i, \ldots, V_m^i)'$, $M^i = (M_1^i, \ldots, M_r^i)'$, and $U^k = (U_1^k, \ldots, U_m^k)'$. The interpretations of the variables used in the above equations are as follows: X_i is the amount of the ith commodity, M_k the amount of the kth intermediate good, V_j^i the amount of the jth primary factor used in the production of the ith commodity, U_j^k the amount of the jth primary factor used in the production of the kth intermediate good, and M_k^i the amount of the kth intermediate good used in the production of the ith commodity. The resource constraints of the intermediate goods and the primary factors are, respectively,

$$(3) \qquad\qquad \sum_{i=1}^{n} M^i \leqq M$$

where $M \equiv (M_1, \ldots, M_r)'$, and

$$(4) \qquad\qquad \sum_{i=1}^{n} V^i + \sum_{k=1}^{r} U^k \leqq V$$

where $V \equiv (V_1, \ldots, V_m)'$ and V_i, $i = 1, \ldots, m$, are given and fixed. The production-possibility set is defined as

$$S \equiv \{X = (X_1, \ldots, X_n) \in R_+^n : X_i \leqq F^i(V^i, M^i), i = 1, \ldots, n,$$

$$M_k = G^k(U^k), k = 1, \ldots, r, \sum_{i=1}^{n} M^i \leqq M, \sum_{i=1}^{n} V^i + \sum_{k=1}^{r} U^k \leqq V\}$$

---

[1] See, for example, Batra and Casas (1973), Flam (1979), and Schweinberger (1975a,b).

The production functions are restricted in the following way.

(i) F^i is strictly quasi-concave as well as linear-homogeneous with respect to all variables.

(ii) G^k is strictly quasi-concave as well as linear-homogeneous with respect to all variables.

(iii) $\partial F^i/\partial V_j^i > 0$ and $\partial F^i/\partial M_k^i \geq 0$ for all i, j, and k.

(iv) $\partial G^k/\partial U_j^k > 0$ for all k and j.

(v)   In any production sector, at least one primary factor is needed for positive output.

3.   ANALYSIS

To begin with, we propose two lemmas.

LEMMA 1:   (a) At any point in the surface of S, (1)–(4) hold with equality. (b) The surface of S slopes negatively everywhere.

Proof.   (a) is clear from (iii) and (v). To verify (b), suppose that there is a point X^* in the surface such that $\tilde{X}$ exists in S and satisfies $\tilde{X} \geq X^*$. Then, for some i, $\tilde{X}_i > X_i^*$. Let us now eliminate some positive primary input from the ith production sector [such an input exists by the assumption (v)], distributing the eliminated amount to the other production sectors. By this method we can construct a new feasible production point X such that $X > X^*$. This contradicts the presumption that X^* is the surface.   ■

LEMMA 2:   The set S is convex.

Proof.   Consider any two distinct points $\overline{X}$ and $\overline{\overline{X}} \in S$. For $\theta \in (0, 1)$, it follows from the concavity of F^i that

$$\theta F^i(\overline{V}^i, \overline{M}^i) + (1 - \theta)F^i(\overline{\overline{V}}^i, \overline{\overline{M}}^i)$$

$$\leq F^i(\theta\overline{V}^i + (1 - \theta)\overline{\overline{V}}^i, \theta\overline{M}^i + (1 - \theta)\overline{\overline{M}}^i), \qquad i = 1, \ldots, n$$

and, from the concavity of G^i, that

$$(5) \qquad \theta G^k(\overline{U}^k) + (1 - \theta)G^k(\overline{\overline{U}}^k)$$

$$\leq G^k(\theta\overline{U}^k + (1 - \theta)\overline{\overline{U}}^k) \equiv \tilde{M}_k, \qquad k = 1, \ldots, r$$

Hence, for $\tilde{U}^k \equiv \theta\overline{U}^k + (1 - \theta)\overline{\overline{U}}^k, \tilde{M}^i \equiv \theta\overline{M}^i + (1 - \theta)\overline{\overline{M}}^i$, and $\tilde{V}^i \equiv \theta\overline{V}^i + (1 - \theta)\overline{\overline{V}}^i$, we have, from (5),

$$\theta\overline{X}^i + (1 - \theta)\overline{\overline{X}}^i \leq F^i(\tilde{V}^i, \tilde{M}^i), \qquad i = 1, \ldots, n$$

and

$$\sum_{i=1}^{n} \tilde{M}_k^i = \theta \sum_{i=1}^{n} \overline{M}_k^i + (1 - \theta) \sum_{i=1}^{n} \overline{\overline{M}}_k^i$$

$$\leqq \theta \overline{M}_k + (1 - \theta) \overline{\overline{M}}_k \leqq \tilde{M}_k, \qquad k = 1, \ldots, r$$

Moreover,

$$\sum_{i=1}^{n} V^i + \sum_{r=1}^{k} U^k$$

$$= \theta \sum_{i=1}^{n} V^i + (1 - \theta) \sum_{i=1}^{n} V^i + \theta \sum_{k=1}^{r} U^k + (1 - \theta) \sum_{k=1}^{r} U^k$$

$$= \theta(\sum_{i=1}^{n} V^i + \sum_{k=1}^{r} U^k) + (1 - \theta)(\sum_{i=1}^{n} V^i + \sum_{k=1}^{r} U^k) \leqq V$$

Therefore,

$$\theta X + (1 - \theta)X \in S. \quad \blacksquare$$

Now we are in a position to prove the following:

THEOREM: Let $\tilde{X}$ be any strictly positive vector point. Then the surface of the production set contains a q-dimensional flat embracing $\tilde{X}$ if and only if the rank of the matrix $\tilde{V} + \tilde{U}\tilde{D}^{-1}\tilde{M}$ is exactly $n - q$, where

$$\tilde{V} = \begin{bmatrix} \tilde{V}_1^1 & \cdots & \tilde{V}_1^n \\ \vdots & & \vdots \\ \tilde{V}_m^1 & \cdots & \tilde{V}_m^n \end{bmatrix}, \qquad \tilde{U} = \begin{bmatrix} \tilde{U}_1^1 & \cdots & \tilde{U}_1^{\tilde{r}} \\ \vdots & & \vdots \\ \tilde{U}_m^1 & \cdots & \tilde{U}_m^{\tilde{r}} \end{bmatrix}$$

$$\tilde{M} = \begin{bmatrix} \tilde{M}_1^1 & \cdots & \tilde{M}_1^n \\ \vdots & & \vdots \\ \tilde{M}_{\tilde{r}}^1 & \cdots & \tilde{M}_{\tilde{r}}^n \end{bmatrix}, \qquad \tilde{D} = \begin{bmatrix} \tilde{M}_1 & & 0 \\ & \ddots & \\ 0 & & \tilde{M}_{\tilde{r}} \end{bmatrix}$$

and only the first $\tilde{r}$ intermediate-good industries are active at $\tilde{X}$.

Proof. To apply the K–K–U proposition [the proposition proved in Kemp *et al.* (1978)], the kth intermediate good is treated as the $(n + k)$th final good for $k - 1, \ldots, r$, so that the net output of the $(n + k)$th industry is always equal to zero. It follows that the inter-

industrial flow matrix (a_{ij}) is of order $(n + r) \times (n + r)$ and such that

$$a_{ij} = \begin{cases} M_k^j & \text{for} \quad i = n + k, \quad k = 1, \ldots, r, \quad j = 1, \ldots, n \\ 0 & \text{otherwise} \end{cases}$$

where a_{ij} is the input of the ith good into the jth industry.

(Sufficiency) In view of the assumption, we have q linearly independent vectors $d^{(h)}$, $h = 1, \ldots, q$, such that

(6) $$(\tilde{V} + \tilde{U}\tilde{D}^{-1}\tilde{M})d^{(h)} = 0$$

Let $\tilde{e}^{(h)} = \tilde{D}^{-1}\tilde{M}d^{(h)}$. Then

(7) $$\tilde{V}d^{(h)} + \tilde{U}\tilde{e}^{(h)} = 0$$

where $(d^{(h)}, \tilde{e}^{(h)})' = (d_1^{(h)}, \ldots, d_n^{(h)}, e_1^{(h)}, \ldots, e_{\tilde{r}}^{(h)})'$, $h = 1, \ldots, q$, are linearly independent. Therefore, applying the K–K–U proposition to our model, we obtain a q-dimensional flat in the final and pure intermediate goods surface.

We obtain also

(8) $$\begin{bmatrix} X^{(h)} - \tilde{X} \\ M^{(h)} - \tilde{M} \end{bmatrix} = \delta_h \begin{bmatrix} \tilde{X}_1 & & 0 & & & \\ & \ddots & & & 0 & \\ 0 & & \tilde{X}_n & & & \\ \hline \tilde{M}_1^1 & \cdots & -\tilde{M}_1^n & \tilde{M}_1 & & 0 \\ \vdots & & \vdots & & \ddots & \\ \tilde{M}_{\tilde{r}}^1 & \cdots & -\tilde{M}_{\tilde{r}}^n & 0 & & \tilde{M}_{\tilde{r}} \end{bmatrix} \begin{bmatrix} d^{(h)} \\ \tilde{e}^{(h)} \end{bmatrix},$$

$$h = 1, \ldots, q$$

from the proof process of the K–K–U proposition, where $(X^{(h)}, M^{(h)})$ is a point in the q-dimensional flat. However, (8) yields

$$M^{(h)} - \tilde{M} = -\tilde{M}d^{(h)} + \tilde{D}\tilde{e}^{(h)}, \qquad h = 1, \ldots, q$$

which, given the definition of $\tilde{e}^{(h)}$, implies that $M^{(h)} = \tilde{M}$, $h = 1, \ldots, q$. Hence the q-dimensional flat in the final and pure-intermediate goods surface appears also in the final-commodity surface.

(Necessity) Applying the K–K–U proposition to our model, we find that the rank of the matrix $[\tilde{V}, \tilde{U}]$ is $m + r - q$. Therefore we have q linearly independent vectors $(d^{(h)}, \tilde{e}^{(h)})' = (d_1^{(h)}, \ldots, d_n^{(h)}, e_1^{(h)}, \ldots, e_{\tilde{r}}^{(h)})'$ such that

(9) $$\tilde{V}d^{(h)} + \tilde{U}\tilde{e}^{(h)} = 0, \qquad h = 1, \ldots, q$$

From the proof of the K–K–U proposition, we have Eq. (8) for a production point $(X^{(h)}, M^{(h)})$ in a flat of the frontier. However, $M^{(h)} - \tilde{M}$ is equal to zero since the net outputs of the pure intermediate goods are always equal to zero. Hence

(10) $\qquad \tilde{M}d^{(h)} = \tilde{D}\tilde{e}^{(h)} \qquad$ or $\qquad \tilde{e}^{(h)} = \tilde{D}^{-1}\tilde{M}d^{(h)}$

Substituting (10) into (9) gives

$$(\tilde{V} + \tilde{U}\tilde{D}^{-1}\tilde{M})d^{(h)} = 0, \qquad h = 1, \ldots, q$$

Now if $d^{(h)}, h = 1, \ldots, q$, are linearly independent, $(d^{(h)}, \tilde{e}^{(h)})', h = 1, \ldots, q$, are also linearly independent in view of (9), which is a contradiction. Therefore the rank of the matrix $(\tilde{V} + \tilde{U}\tilde{D}^{-1}\tilde{M})$ is at most $m - q$. If the rank is less than $n - q$, then, by sufficiency, we have a flat of higher dimension than q, which is a contradiction. ∎

Remark 1. The activity $(\hat{V}^i_1, \ldots, \hat{V}^i_m, \hat{M}^i_1, \ldots, \hat{M}^i_r)$ producing a unit of the ith final commodity and the activity $(\hat{U}^k_1, \ldots, \hat{U}^k_m)$ producing a unit of the kth intermediate good are constant at any point in a flat of the surface. This is easily seen by following the proof process. Therefore, in particular, if at some point in the flat the kth intermediate good is not used in the production of any final commodity, then it is never used in the production of any final commodity at any point of the flat. Conversely, if the intermediate good is used at some point of the flat, then it has to be used at every point of the flat.

Remark 2. The meaning of the matrix $\tilde{V} + \tilde{U}\tilde{D}^{-1}\tilde{M}$ is easily understood if we pay attention to each factor of the matrix. After calculation, we obtain the (j, i)th element of the matrix as

$$\sum_{k=1}^{\tilde{r}} \tilde{U}^k_j(\tilde{M}^i_k/\tilde{M}_k)$$

This can be interpreted as the amount of the jth primary factor used in the production of the intermediate goods that are used in the production of the ith final commodity. Therefore, the (j, i)th element of $\tilde{V} + \tilde{U}\tilde{D}^{-1}\tilde{M}$ is the total amount of the jth primary factor used in the production of the ith final commodity both directly and indirectly through intermediate goods.

Remark 3. Suppose that $m = 1$. Then the rank of the matrix $V + UD^{-1}M$ is 1 everywhere in the surface, which implies that the whole surface is an $(n - 1)$-dimensional flat. Accordingly, by Remark

1, the activity $(\hat{V}^i, \hat{M}_1^i, \ldots, \hat{M}_r^i)$, for a unit production, is unchanged in every final-commodity production sector and in the whole surface. This can be referred to as the nonsubstitutability of pure intermediate goods.

REFERENCES

Batra, R. N., and Casas, F. R. (1973). Intermediate products and the pure theory of international trade: A neo-Heckscher–Ohlin framework. *American Economic Review* **63,** 297–311.

Flam, H. (1979). The Rybczynski theorem in a model with non-traded goods and indecomposable interindustry flows. *International Economic Review* **20,** 661–670.

Kemp, M. C., Khang, C., and Uekawa, Y. (1978). On the flatness of the transformation surface. *Journal of International Economics* **8,** 537–542 (reprinted as Chapter 2 in this volume).

Kemp, M. C., Manning, R., Nishimura, K., and Tawada, M. (1980). On the shape of the single-country and world commodity-substitution and factor-substitution surfaces under conditions of joint production. *Journal of International Economics* **10,** 395–404 (reprinted as Chapter 5 in this volume).

Khang, C. (1971). The strict convexity of the transformation surface in case of linear homogeneous production functions. *Econometrica* **39,** 857–858.

Khang, C., and Uekawa, Y. (1973). The production possibility set in a model allowing interindustry flows: The necessary and sufficient conditions for its strict convexity. *Journal of International Economics* **3,** 283–290.

Schweinberger, A. (1975a). Pure traded intermediate products and the Heckscher–Ohlin theorem. *American Economic Review* **65,** 634–643.

Schweinberger, A. (1975b). Comparative advantage and intermediate products. *Economic Record* **51,** 191–202.

Tawada, M. (1980). The production-possibility set with public intermediate goods. *Econometrica* **48,** 1005–1012 (reprinted as Chapter 9 in this volume).

DEPARTMENT OF ECONOMICS
KOBE UNIVERSITY OF COMMERCE
TARUMI, KOBE
JAPAN

4

On the shape of the world production frontier*

MAKOTO TAWADA

1. INTRODUCTION

In many branches of trade theory, but notably in the analysis of trade gains, it is common to assign a central role to the world production frontier. Yet surprisingly little is known about the properties of the frontier. We know from countless textbooks that, in the Torrens–Ricardo one-factor, two-countries, two-commodities case, the frontier is weakly concave, consisting of two straight-line segments. And we know from Lerner (1932) that in the Heckscher–Ohlin two-factors, two-countries, two-commodities case, the frontier is strictly concave if in each country the two industries differ in factor intensity. Recently the Heckscher–Ohlin model has been extended to allow for the possibility that one of the two factors is internationally mobile (see Kemp, 1966; Jones, 1967; Inada and Kemp, 1969; Chipman, 1971; Uekawa, 1972). In particular, it has been shown by Chipman that the world production frontier may contain a flat segment.

In the present chapter we consider the general case in which countries, factors, and commodities are arbitrary in number and in which

* This is a part of my Ph.D. dissertation presented to the University of New South Wales. I would like to express my deep gratitude to Professor M. C. Kemp for his kind instruction and suggestions.

25

any subset of the commodities and any subset of the factors may be internationally mobile. In Section 2 we derive a condition that is necessary and sufficient for the world production frontier to contain a ρ-dimensional flat. The earlier work of Lerner, Chipman, and Uekawa falls into place; and the same is true of the recent closed-economy analyses of Khang (1971), Khang and Uekawa (1973), and Kemp et al. (1978), to which the present essay is closely related. In a series of final remarks we note several extensions of our finding as well as several specializations thereof.

2. ANALYSIS

We consider a world economy composed of r countries, each endowed with m primary factors of production and able to produce n commodities. In each industry in each country some or all of the produced commodities may serve as intermediate inputs. Thus the ith production function of the kth country is

$$(1) \qquad y_i^k = f^{ki}(v^{ki}, x^{ki}), \qquad k = 1, \ldots, r, \quad i = 1, \ldots, n$$

where $v^{ki} \equiv (v_{i1}^k, \ldots, v_{im}^k)$ and $x^{ki} \equiv (x_{i1}^k, \ldots, x_{in}^k)$ are the vectors of primary and intermediate inputs, respectively. The production functions may differ from country to country but are subject to the following restrictions:

(A1) Each f^{ki} is homogeneous of degree one and strictly quasi-concave with respect to all of its arguments.

(A2) Each f^{ki} has continuous first-order partial derivatives with respect to all of its arguments. Each derivative is either identically zero or identically positive.

The jth primary factor is internationally immobile if $1 \leq j \leq m^0$ and mobile otherwise. The resource constraints are, therefore,

$$(2) \qquad \sum_{i=1}^{n} v_{ij}^k \leq \bar{v}_j^k, \qquad j = 1, \ldots, m_0, \quad k = 1, \ldots, r$$

$$(3) \qquad \sum_{k=1}^{r} \sum_{i=1}^{n} v_{ij}^k \leq \bar{v}_j, \qquad j = m_0 + 1, \ldots, m$$

where $\bar{v}_j^k$ is the kth country's endowment of the jth primary factor and $\bar{v}_j \equiv \sum_{k=1}^{r} \bar{v}_j^k$.

For the time being it is assumed that all n produced goods are internationally mobile. It follows that the net production of any ith commodity in any kth country, say $z_i^k \equiv yki - \sum_{j=1}^{n} x_{ji}^k$, may be negative and that the world net production set is

$$Z \equiv \{z \equiv (z_1, \ldots, z_n) \in R_+^n : (1)-(3) \text{ are satisfied}\}$$

where $z_i \equiv \sum_{k=1}^{r} z_i^k$, $i = 1, \ldots, n$. The world production frontier is the upper boundary of Z.

LEMMA: Z is convex.

Proof.   Let $z^l \in Z$, $l = 0, 1$. Then

$$(4) \qquad \sum_{i=1}^{n} v_{ij}^{kl} \leq \bar{v}_j^k, \qquad j = 1, \ldots, m_0, \quad k = 1, \ldots, r$$

$$(5) \qquad \sum_{k=1}^{r} \sum_{i=1}^{n} v_{ij}^{kl} < \bar{v}_j, \qquad j = m_0 + 1, \ldots, m$$

Let $z_i^\theta \equiv \theta z_i^0 + (1 - \theta)z_i^1$ for some $\theta \in (0, 1)$. Then

$$z_i^\theta = \sum_{k=1}^{r} \{\theta z_i^{k0} + (1 - \theta)z_i^{k1}\}$$

$$= \sum_{k=1}^{r} \{\theta y_i^{k0} + (1 - \theta)y_i^{k1} - \sum_{j=1}^{n} (\theta x_{ji}^{k0} + (1 - \theta)x_{ji}^{k1})\}$$

and, from the concavity of f^{ki},

$$(6) \qquad z_i^\theta \leq \sum_{k=1}^{r} \{f^{ki}(\theta v^{ki0} + (1 - \theta)v^{ki1}, \theta x^{ki0} + (1 - \theta)x^{ki1})$$

$$- \sum_{j=1}^{n} (\theta x_{ji}^{k0} + (1 - \theta)x_{ji}^{k1})\}$$

On the other hand, from (4) and (5),

$$(7) \qquad \sum_{i=1}^{n} \{\theta v_{ij}^{k0} + (1 - \theta)v_{ij}^{k1}\} \leq \bar{v}_j^k, \qquad j = 1, \ldots, m_0, \quad k = 1, \ldots, r$$

$$(8) \qquad \sum_{k=1}^{r} \sum_{i=1}^{n} \{\theta v_{ij}^{k0} + (1 - \theta)v_{ij}^{k1}\} \leq \bar{v}_j, \qquad j = m_0 + 1, \ldots, m$$

From (6)–(8), $z^\theta \in Z$.   ∎

PROPOSITION: Let $\hat{z} \equiv (\hat{z}_1, \ldots, \hat{z}_n) > 0$ be a point on the world production frontier and let an associated factor allocation be described by the matrices

$$A^k \equiv \begin{bmatrix} \hat{v}^k_{11} & \cdots & \hat{v}^k_{n1} \\ \vdots & & \vdots \\ \hat{v}^k_{1m_0} & \cdots & \hat{v}^k_{nm_0} \end{bmatrix}, \qquad k = 1, \ldots, r$$

$$B^k \equiv \begin{bmatrix} \hat{v}^k_{1(m_0+1)} & \cdots & \hat{v}^k_{n(m_0+1)} \\ \vdots & & \vdots \\ \hat{v}^k_{1m} & \cdots & \hat{v}^k_{nm} \end{bmatrix}, \qquad k = 1, \ldots, r$$

$$D^k \equiv \begin{bmatrix} \hat{y}^k_1 - \hat{x}^k_{11} & -\hat{x}^k_{21} & \cdots & -\hat{x}^k_{n1} \\ \hat{x}^k_{12} & \hat{y}^k_2 - \hat{x}^k_{22} & \cdots & -\hat{x}^k_{n2} \\ \vdots & \vdots & & \vdots \\ -\hat{x}^k_{1n} & -\hat{x}^k_{2n} & \cdots & \hat{y}^k_n - \hat{x}^k_{nn} \end{bmatrix}, \qquad k = 1, \ldots, r$$

Then there exists a ρ-dimensional flat that contains $\hat{z}$ and lies in the frontier if and only if the subset

$$S \equiv \{ \sum_{k=1}^{r} D^k d^k \in R^n : A^k d^k = 0, \, k = 1, \ldots, r, \text{ and } \sum_{k=1}^{r} B^k d^k = 0 \}$$

contains exactly ρ linearly independent vectors, where

$$d^k \equiv \begin{bmatrix} d^k_1 \\ \vdots \\ d^k_n \end{bmatrix}, \qquad k = 1, \ldots, r$$

Proof. (Necessity) Suppose that there exists a nondegenerate line segment that lies in the frontier and contains $\hat{z}$. Let the segment be (z^0, z^1), where $z^l \neq \hat{z}$ and $z^l \equiv (z^l_1, \ldots, z^l_n)$, $z^l_i \equiv \sum_{k=1}^{r} z^{kl}_i$, $z^{kl}_i \equiv y^{kl}_i - \sum_{j=1}^{n} x^{kl}_{ji}$, and $y^{kl}_i = f^{ki}(v^{kil}, x^{kil})$ for $k = 1, \ldots, r$, $i = 1, \ldots, n$, and $l = 0, 1$. From (A2) and the fact that z^l lies in the frontier,

(9) $$\sum_{i=1}^{n} v^{kl}_{ij} = \bar{v}^k_j, \qquad j = 1, \ldots, m_0, \quad l = 0, 1$$

(10) $$\sum_{k=1}^{r} \sum_{i=1}^{n} v^{kl}_{ij} = \bar{v}_j, \qquad j = m_0 + 1, \ldots, m, \quad l = 0, 1$$

Since $\hat{z}$ lies in the line segment (z^0, z^1), there exist unique $\alpha > 0$ and $\beta > 0$ such that $\alpha + \beta = 1$ and $\hat{z} = \alpha z^0 + \beta z^1$. From the concavity of f^{ki},

(11) $\quad \alpha z_i^{k0} + \beta z_i^{k1} = \alpha y_i^{k0} + \beta y_i^{k1} - \sum_{j=1}^{n} (\alpha x_{ji}^{k0} + \beta_{ji}^{k1})$

$$\leq f^{ki}(\alpha v^{ki0} + \beta v^{ki1}, \alpha x^{ki0} + \beta x^{ki1}) - \sum_{j=1}^{n} (\alpha x_{ji}^{k0} + \beta x_{ji}^{k1})$$

Let $\hat{v}^{ki} \equiv \alpha v^{ki0} + \beta v^{ki1}$ and $\hat{x}^{ki} \equiv \alpha x^{ki0} + \beta x^{ki1}$. From (9) and (10),

(12) $\qquad\qquad \sum_{i=1}^{n} \hat{v}_{ij}^{k} = \bar{v}_j^k, \qquad j = 1, \ldots, m_0$

(13) $\qquad\qquad \sum_{k=1}^{r} \sum_{i=1}^{n} \hat{v}_{ij}^{k} = \bar{v}_j, \qquad j = m_0 + 1, \ldots, m$

That is, the $\hat{v}^{ki}$, $k = 1, \ldots, r$ and $i = 1, \ldots, n$, are feasible. In view of (11), therefore,

$$\alpha z_i^{k0} + \beta z_i^{k1} = f^{ki}(\alpha v^{ki0} + \beta v^{ki1}, \alpha x^{ki0} + \beta x^{ki1}) - \sum_{j=1}^{n} (\alpha x_{ji}^{k0} + \beta x_{ji}^{k1})$$

or, since $\hat{z}$ is in the frontier,

(14) $\qquad\qquad \alpha y_i^{k0} + \beta y_i^{k1} = f^{ki}(\alpha v^{ki0} + \beta v^{ki1}, \alpha x^{ki0} + \beta x^{ki1})$

From (14) and (A1), there exists a positive scalar a_i^k such that

(15) $\qquad\qquad a_i^k v^{ki0} = v^{ki1} \qquad$ and $\qquad a_i^k x^{ki0} = x^{ki1}$

From (9)–(13) and (15),

(16) $\qquad\qquad \sum_{i=1}^{n} \left(\frac{\alpha + \beta a_i^k - 1}{\alpha + \beta a_i^k} \right) \hat{v}_{ij}^k = 0, \qquad j = 1, \ldots, m_0$

(17) $\qquad \sum_{k=1}^{r} \sum_{i=1}^{n} \left(\frac{\alpha + \beta a_i^k - 1}{\alpha + \beta a_i^k} \right) \hat{v}_{ij}^k = 0, \qquad j = m_0 + 1, \ldots, m$

Now let $i^*(k)$ be indices such that $y_i^k = 0$. Then $\hat{v}^{ki^*(k)} = 0$, and (16) and (17) can be rewritten as

(18) $\qquad\qquad \sum_{\substack{i=1 \\ i \neq i^*(k)}}^{n} \left(\frac{\alpha + \beta a_i^k - 1}{\alpha + \beta a_i^k} \right) \hat{v}_{ij}^k = 0, \qquad j = 1, \ldots, m_0$

and

(19) $\qquad \sum_{k=1}^{r} \sum_{\substack{i=1 \\ i \neq i^*(k)}}^{n} \left(\frac{\alpha + \beta a_i^k - 1}{\alpha + \beta a_i^k} \right) \hat{v}_{ij}^k = 0, \qquad j = m_0 + 1, \ldots, m$

Now $\hat{z}$ is on the frontier; hence, for any pair (k^*, i^*) such that $\hat{y}_{i*}^{k*} = 0$, $\hat{v}^{k*i*} = 0 = \hat{x}^{k*i*}$ and, for $l = 0, 1, v^{k*i*l} = 0 = x^{k*i*l}$. It follows that if all a_i^k associated with positive $\hat{y}_i^k$ are equal to unity, then $v^{ki0} = v^{ki1}$ and $x^{ki0} = x^{ki1}$, contradicting the assumption that $z^0 \neq z^1$. Thus we may be sure that there is at least one pair (k, i) such that $a_i^k \neq 1$ and $\hat{y}_i^k > 0$, so that $(\alpha + \beta a_i^k - 1)/(\alpha + \beta a_i^k)$ in (18) and (19) is nonzero. We therefore define

(20)
$$d_i^k = \begin{cases} \dfrac{\alpha + \beta a_i^k - 1}{\alpha + \beta a_i^k} & \text{if } \hat{y}_i^k > 0 \\ 0 & \text{if } \hat{y}_i^k = 0 \end{cases}$$

and notice that such d_i^k satisfy

$$A^k d^k = 0 \quad \text{and} \quad \sum_{k=1}^{r} B^k d^k = 0$$

Now we have

$$z_i^{k0} \equiv f^{ki}(v^{ki0}, x^{ki0}) - \sum_{j=1}^{n} x_{ji}^{k0}$$

$$= \frac{1}{\alpha + \beta a_i^k} f^{ki}(\hat{v}^{ki}, \hat{x}^{ki}) - \sum_{j=1}^{n} \frac{1}{\alpha + \beta a_j^k} \hat{x}_{ji}^k$$

Hence, for d_j^k defined by (20),

$$\hat{z}_i^k - z_i^{k0} = d_i^k \hat{y}_i^k - \sum_{j=1}^{n} d_j^k \hat{x}_{ji}^k$$

Since $\alpha > 0$ and $\beta > 0, z^0 \neq \hat{z}$. Hence, summing over k,

$$\sum_{k=1}^{r} (\hat{z}_i^k - z_i^{k0}) = \sum_{k=1}^{r} (d_i^k \hat{y}_i^k - \sum_{j=1}^{n} d_j^k \hat{x}_{ji}^k) \neq 0 \quad \text{for some } i$$

which implies that

$$\hat{z} - z^0 = \sum_{k=1}^{r} D^k d^k \neq 0$$

By assumption we have ρ linearly independent vectors $\hat{z} - z^h$, $h = 1$, ..., ρ, such that the line segment $(\hat{z}, z^h)$ is on the frontier. Hence there are ρ linearly independent vectors in S.

(Sufficiency)   Suppose that there exist d_i^k, not all zero, such that

$$A^k d^k = 0, \qquad k = 1, \ldots, r$$

$$\sum_{k=1}^{r} B^k d^k = 0$$

$$\sum_{k=1}^{r} D^k d^k \neq 0$$

Now choose a nonzero, positive or negative scalar α such that $1 + \alpha d_i^k > 0$ for all such d_i^k, and define

(21)
$$\bar{v}_{ij}^k \equiv (1 + \alpha d_i^k) \hat{v}_{ij}^k$$
$$\bar{x}_{ij}^k \equiv (1 + \alpha d_i^k) \hat{x}_{ij}^k$$

Then

(22)
$$\sum_{i=1}^{n} \bar{v}_{ij}^k = \sum_{i=1}^{n} \hat{v}_{ij}^k, \qquad j = 1, \ldots, m_0$$
$$\sum_{k=1}^{r} \sum_{i=1}^{n} \bar{v}_{ij}^k = \sum_{k=1}^{r} \sum_{i=1}^{n} \hat{v}_{ij}^k, \qquad j = m_0 + 1, \ldots, m$$

Moreover,

(23) $$\bar{z}_i^k \equiv f^{ki}(\bar{v}^{ki}, \bar{x}^{ki}) - \sum_{j=1}^{n} \bar{x}_{ji}^k$$

$$= (1 + \alpha d_i^k) f^{ki}(\hat{v}^{ki}, \hat{x}^{ki}) - \sum_{j=1}^{n} (1 + \alpha d_j^k) \hat{x}_{ji}^k$$

$$= \hat{z}_i^k + \alpha (d_i^k \hat{y}_i^k - \sum_{j=1}^{n} d_j^k \hat{x}_{ji}^k), \qquad i = 1, \ldots, n, \quad k = 1, \ldots, r$$

By assumption, $\sum_{k=1}^{r} \hat{z}_i^k \equiv \hat{z}_i > 0$. Hence, for sufficiently small α, $\sum_{k=1}^{r} \bar{z}_i^k \equiv \bar{z}_i > 0$ and $\bar{z} \equiv (\bar{z}_1, \ldots, \bar{z}_n) \in Z$.

Let $\hat{p} \equiv (\hat{p}_1, \ldots, \hat{p}_n) > 0$ be a vector of shadow prices associated with $\hat{z}$. Then, from (23) and the convexity of Z,

(24) $$0 \geq \hat{p}(\bar{z} - \hat{z})$$

$$= \alpha \sum_{i=1}^{n} \hat{p}_i \sum_{k=1}^{r} (d_i^k \hat{y}_i^k - \sum_{j=1}^{n} d_j^k \hat{x}_{ji}^k)$$

Now α can be positive or negative; hence

$$\hat{p}\bar{z} = \hat{p}\hat{z}$$

and $\bar{z}$ is efficient. Since Z is convex, the line segment $(\hat{z}, \bar{z})$ is contained in Z; in fact, the segment lies in the frontier and has associated with it the shadow-price vector $\hat{p}$.

It must be shown that $\hat{z} \neq \bar{z}$. If we assume that $\hat{z} = \bar{z}$, then, from (23),

$$\sum_{k=1}^{r} (d_1^k \hat{y}_1^k - \sum_{j=1}^{n} d_j^k \hat{x}_{ji}^k) = 0$$

contradicting the assumption that $\sum_{k=1}^{n} D^k d^k \neq 0$. Therefore $\hat{z} \neq \bar{z}$. Now by assumption there are ρ linearly independent vectors $\sum_{k=1}^{n} D^k d^k$ in S. In view of (23), therefore, we can construct ρ linearly independent vectors $\hat{z} - \bar{z}$, where the line segment $(\hat{z}, \bar{z})$ is on the frontier. Hence there exists a ρ-dimensional flat on the frontier. ∎

The above proposition has an immediate corollary.

COROLLARY 1: Let $\hat{z} > 0$ be a point on the world production frontier. Then there exists a nondegenerate line segment which contains $\hat{z}$ and lies in the frontier if and only if there exist r vectors $d^k, k = 1, \ldots, r$, such that

(ia) $A^k d^k = 0, k = 1, \ldots, r$,
(ib) $\sum_{k=1}^{r} B^k d^k = 0$,
(ii) $\sum_{k=1}^{r} D^k d^k \neq 0$,

where A^k, B^k, and D^k are as defined in the proposition.

We offer without proof another proposition relating to the steady states of economies with durable intermediate inputs. This proposition may be compared with Theorem 2' of Kemp et al. (1978).

COROLLARY 2: Suppose now that each of the n products may serve as a perfectly durable input to some or all industries, that in each country all m primary factors grow at the common rate $g, g \geq 0$, and that the own-rate of return to any capital good actually produced is equal to g. Suppose also that assumptions (A1) and (A2), suitably reinterpreted, continue to be satisfied. Let $\hat{z} > 0$ be a point on the steady-state world net production frontier. Then the frontier contains a ρ-dimensional flat if and only if there are ρ linearly independent vectors in subset S of the proposition.

3. EXTENSIONS AND SPECIALIZATIONS

We proceed by means of a succession of remarks that indicate extensions or specializations of the proposition. The first two remarks indicate extensions, the remaining remarks specializations.

Remark 1. It has been assumed that all n produced commodities are tradable. However, it is easy to allow for the possibility that any number of commodities n_0, $n_0 \leqq n$, are tradable. Indeed, the proposition is valid whatever the number of traded commodities provided only that all nontraded commodities are everywhere produced in positive net amounts, that is, provided that $z_i^k > 0$ for all k and for $i = n_0 + 1, \ldots, n$.

Remark 2. Consider a point $\hat{z}$ in the world production frontier and the international allocation of primary factors associated with that point. (The allocation need not be unique.) Suppose that, given that allocation, the production possibility frontier of the kth country contains a g_k-dimensional flat. Then, from the proposition of Kemp, Khang, and Uekawa, at $\hat{z}$ and in the kth country there are exactly $n_k - g_k$ linearly independent vectors of primary inputs, where n_k is the number of active industries in the kth country. Therefore, there exist g_k linearly independent vectors $c^k(1), \ldots, c^k(g_k)$, $k = 1, \ldots, r$, satisfying the condition that

$$A^k C^k(l) = 0 \quad \text{and} \quad B^k C^k(l) = 0, \quad l = 1, \ldots, g_k, \quad k = 1, \ldots, r$$

Now we can construct $\sum_{k=1}^{r} g_k$ linearly independent vectors

$$d^k(l) \equiv (0^{1'}, \ldots, 0^{k-1'} C^k(l)' 0^{k+1'}, \ldots, 0^{r'})', \quad l = 1, \ldots, g_k, \quad k = 1, \ldots, r$$

where 0^i is the n-dimensional null vector. Following the proof of Kemp, Khang, and Uekawa, it can be shown that $D^k C^k(1), \ldots, D^k C^k(g_k)$ are linearly independent. In view of our own proposition, it follows that the degree of the flatness of the world production frontier at $\hat{z}$ is not less than $\max\{g_1, g_2, \ldots, g_r\}$.

Suppose that all factors are internationally immobile. Then the condition $\sum_{k=1}^{r} B^k d^k = 0$ disappears and we can construct d only by combining the vectors $C^k(l_k)$, $k = 1, \ldots, r$, $l_k \in \{1, \ldots, g_k\}$ with n-dimensional null vectors. Clearly, any vector $\sum_{k=1}^{r} \delta_k D^k C^k(l_k)$, where δ_k is a scalar taking the value 1 or 0, is linearly dependent on the $\sum_{k=1}^{r} g_k$ vectors $D^k C^k(l_k)$. It follows that if all primary factors are internationally immobile, the degree of the flatness of the world production frontier is the rank of the matrix

$$[D^1 C^1 \quad D^2 C^2 \quad \cdots \quad D^n C^r]$$

where $C^k \equiv (C^k(1), \ldots, C^k(g_k))$.

Remark 3. If the vectors d^k satisfying conditions (i) and (ii) of Corollary 1 are such that $d^k \neq 0$ for $k = 1, \ldots, r_0$ and $d^k = 0$ for $k = r_0 + 1, \ldots, r$, then, as the world production point moves along the line segment, any movement of factors and any changes in outputs are confined to the first r_0 countries. In particular, if $r_0 = 1$, all factor movements and output changes are confined to the first country.

Remark 4. If $r = 1$, the world economy reduces to a single closed economy and, removing the country superscripts, the subset S of the proposition reduces to

$$S \equiv \{Dd : Ad = 0 \text{ and } Bd = 0\}$$

However, $\hat{z} \equiv (\hat{z}_1, \ldots, \hat{z}_n) > 0$, where $\hat{z}_i = \hat{y}_i - \sum_{j=1}^{n} \hat{x}_{ji}$, $i = 1, \ldots, n$; hence D has a dominant diagonal and thus has full rank. Hence $Dd(1), \ldots, Dd(\rho)$, are linearly independent if and only if vectors $d(1), \ldots, d(\rho)$ are linearly independent. Moreover, there are linearly independent vectors $d(1), \ldots, d(\rho)$ such that $Ad(l) = 0$ and $Bd(l) = 0$, $l = 1, \ldots, \rho$, if and only if there are exactly $n - \rho$ linearly independent vectors of primary-factor inputs, which is precisely the condition derived by Kemp *et al.* (1978).

Remark 5. Suppose that $m = n = r = 2$ and that $m_0 = 1$. Then conditions (i) and (ii) of Corollary 1 reduce to the requirement that there exists $d \equiv (d_1^1, d_2^1, d_1^2, d_2^2) \neq 0$ such that

$$(25) \quad \begin{bmatrix} \hat{v}_{11}^1 & \hat{v}_{21}^1 & 0 & 0 \\ 0 & 0 & \hat{v}_{11}^2 & \hat{v}_{21}^2 \\ \hat{v}_{12}^1 & \hat{v}_{22}^1 & \hat{v}_{12}^2 & \hat{v}_{22}^2 \end{bmatrix} \begin{bmatrix} d_1^1 \\ d_2^1 \\ d_1^2 \\ d_2^2 \end{bmatrix} = \begin{bmatrix} 0 \\ 0 \\ 0 \end{bmatrix}$$

and

$$(26) \quad \begin{bmatrix} \hat{y}_1^1 - \hat{x}_{11}^1 & -\hat{x}_{21}^1 \\ -\hat{x}_{12}^1 & \hat{y}_2^1 - \hat{x}_{22}^1 \end{bmatrix} \begin{bmatrix} d_1^1 \\ d_2^1 \end{bmatrix} + \begin{bmatrix} \hat{y}_1^2 - \hat{x}_{11}^2 & -\hat{x}_{21}^2 \\ -\hat{x}_{12}^2 & \hat{y}_2^2 - \hat{x}_{22}^2 \end{bmatrix} \begin{bmatrix} d_1^2 \\ d_2^2 \end{bmatrix} \neq \begin{bmatrix} 0 \\ 0 \end{bmatrix}$$

If there are no interindustrial flows and if both commodities are produced in each country [the case studied by Inada and Kemp (1969),

Chipman (1971), and Uekawa (1972)], then D^k, $k = 1, 2$, are positive-diagonal matrices. It follows that if

$$(27) \qquad \hat{\Delta}^k \equiv \hat{v}_{11}^k \hat{v}_{22}^k - \hat{v}_{12}^k \hat{v}_{21}^k = 0 \qquad \text{for some} \quad k$$

there exists $d^k \neq (0, 0)'$ that, together with $d^l \equiv (0, 0)'$, $l \neq k$, satisfies (25) and (26). That is, if (27) is satisfied at $\hat{z}$, the world production frontier contains a line segment through $\hat{z}$; moreover, movements along the line segment are accompanied by output changes in the kth country only, with no movement of factors between the two countries. This is part (aii) of Chipman's Theorem 2.

Suppose that neither $\hat{\Delta}^1$ nor $\hat{\Delta}^2$ vanishes, so that, from (25),

$$(28) \qquad d_1^1 = -(\hat{v}_{21}^1/\hat{v}_{11}^1)d_2^1 \neq 0$$

$$(29) \qquad d_1^2 = -(\hat{v}_{21}^2/\hat{v}_{11}^2)d_2^2 \neq 0$$

$$(30) \qquad d_2^2 = -(\hat{v}_{11}^2\hat{\Delta}^1/\hat{v}_{11}^1\hat{\Delta}^2)d_2^1 \neq 0$$

If and only if any d that satisfies (28)–(30) also satisfies (26), then the frontier contains a nondegenerate line segment. Following Chipman, we now show that this condition is satisfied if

$$(31) \qquad \frac{\hat{v}_{21}^1}{\hat{y}_2^1} \cdot \frac{\hat{v}_{11}^2}{\hat{y}_1^2} = \frac{\hat{v}_{11}^1}{\hat{y}_1^1} \cdot \frac{\hat{v}_{21}^2}{\hat{y}_2^2}$$

or, equivalently, if

$$(32) \qquad \frac{\hat{v}_{11}^2}{\hat{y}_2^1}\hat{\Delta}^1 = \frac{\hat{v}_{11}^1}{\hat{y}_2^2}\hat{\Delta}^2$$

From (28), (29), and (31),

$$(33) \qquad \hat{y}_1^1 d_1^1 + \hat{y}_1^2 d_1^2 = -(\hat{y}_1^1(\hat{v}_{21}^1/\hat{v}_{11}^1)d_2^1 + \hat{y}_1^2(\hat{v}_{21}^2/\hat{v}_{11}^2)d_2^2)$$
$$= -(\hat{y}_1^1\hat{v}_{21}^1/\hat{y}_2^1\hat{v}_{11}^2)(\hat{y}_2^1 d_2^1 + \hat{y}_2^2 d_2^2)$$

However, from (30) and (32),

$$(34) \qquad \hat{y}_2^1 d_2^1 + \hat{y}_2^2 d_2^2 = 0$$

Hence

$$(35) \qquad \hat{y}_1^1 d_1^1 + \hat{y}_1^2 d_1^2 = 0$$

From (34), (35), and the assumed absence of interindustrial flows, (26) is violated. Thus if (31) or (32) is satisfied, then there is no line segment through $\hat{z}$; and if (31) and (32) do not hold, then (26) is satisfied and the frontier contains a line segment through $\hat{z}$. These conclusions appear as parts (ai) and (b) of Chipman's Theorem 2.

Remark 6. Suppose, following Graham (1948), that $r = n$ and $m = m_0 = 1$, that is, that countries and produced commodities are equal in number and that there is a single, immobile primary factor. It will be shown that the world production frontier contains a non-degenerate line segment through any point $\hat{z} > 0$ if and only if at least one commodity is produced in more than one country. Suppose, then, that at $\hat{z}$ the kth country, $k = 2, \ldots, r$, is specialized to the production of the kth commodity, but that the first country produces both the first and second commodities (so that the second commodity is produced by the first and second countries). We construct a vector d in the following way. The first subvector $d' \equiv (d_1^1, d_2^1)'$ is chosen so that it is nonzero and satisfies

$$A^1 d^1 \equiv v_1^1 d_1^1 + v_2^1 d_2^1 = 0$$

where v_i^k is the positive amount of the primary factor needed to produce y_i^k. All other elements of d are set equal to zero. Clearly, with d chosen in this way,

$$A^k d^k = 0, \qquad k = 1, \ldots, r$$

Moreover

$$\sum_{k=1}^{r} D^k d^k = D^1 d^1 = \begin{bmatrix} (\hat{y}_1^1 - \hat{x}_{11})d_1^1 - \hat{x}_{21}^1 d_2^1 \\ -\hat{x}_{12}^1 d_1^1 + (\hat{y}_2^1 - \hat{x}_{22}^1)d_2^1 \\ -\hat{x}_{13}^1 d_1^1 - \hat{x}_{23}^1 d_2^1 \\ \vdots \\ -\hat{x}_{1n}^1 d_1^1 - \hat{x}_{2n}^1 d_2^1 \end{bmatrix}$$

Now every point on the world production frontier is an equilibrium point of perfect competition. It follows that in every sector profit is zero. Hence the matrix

$$\begin{bmatrix} \hat{y}_1^1 - \hat{x}_{11}^1 & -\hat{x}_{21}^1 \\ -\hat{x}_{12}^1 & \hat{y}_2^1 - \hat{x}_{22}^1 \end{bmatrix}$$

has a dominant diagonal and, therefore, is nonsingular. Hence $\sum_{k=1}^{r} D^k d^k \neq 0$ and conditions (i) and (ii) of Corollary 1 are satisfied. On the other hand, if at $\hat{z}$ each country produces just one commodity, there is no d that satisfies (i) and (ii). Such points of complete specialization are vertices of the frontier.

Suppose that the first country produces the first n_0 commodities, with the kth country being specialized to the production of the kth commodity, $k = 2, \ldots, r$. Then d is chosen so that $d^k = 0, k = 2, \ldots, r$, and so that d^1 satisfies

$$(36) \qquad A^1 d^1 \equiv \sum_{i=1}^{n_0} v_i^1 d_i^1 = 0, \qquad d^1 \neq 0$$

The set of solutions to (36) is an $(n_0 - 1)$-dimensional subspace in R^{n_0}; that is, we can choose $n_0 - 1$ independent vectors $d^{1,1}, \ldots, d^{1,n_0-1}$ satisfying (36). Let $\tilde{D}^1$ be the matrix obtained from D^1 by excluding columns $n_0 + 1, \ldots, n$, and let

$$E \equiv \left[d^{1,1}, \ldots, d^{1,n_0-1} \right]$$

Evidently $\tilde{D}^1$ has rank n_0 and E has rank $n_0 - 1$. Hence $\tilde{D}^1 E$ has rank $n_0 - 1$. Since $\sum_{k=1}^{r} D^k d^k = \tilde{D}^1 d^{1,i}, i - 1, \ldots, n_0 - 1$, and recalling the proposition, the frontier contains an $(n_0 - 1)$-dimensional flat embracing $\hat{z}$.

REFERENCES

Chipman, J. S. (1971). International trade with capital mobility: A substitution theorem. *In* "Trade, Balance of Payments, and Growth" (J. N. Bhagwati, R. W. Jones, R. A. Mundell, and J. Vanek, eds.), pp. 201–237. North-Holland Publ., Amsterdam.

Graham, F. D. (1948). "The Theory of International Values." Princeton Univ. Press, Princeton, New Jersey.

Inada, K., and Kemp, M. C. (1969). International capital movements and the theory of tariffs and trade: Comment. *Quarterly Journal of Economics* **83**, 524–528.

Jones, R. W. (1967). International capital movements and the theory of tariffs and trade. *Quarterly Journal of Economics* **81**, 1–38.

Kemp, M. C. (1966). The gain from international trade and investment: A neo-Heckscher–Ohlin approach. *American Economic Review* **56**, 788–809.

Kemp, M. C., Khang, C., and Uekawa, Y. (1978). On the flatness of the transformation locus. *Journal of International Economics* **8**, 537–542 (reprinted as Chapter 2 of this volume).

Khang, C. (1971). On the strict convexity of the transformation surface in case of linear homogeneous production functions: A general case. *Econometrica* **39**, 857–859.

Khang, C., and Uekawa, Y. (1973). The production possibility set in a model allowing interindustry flows: The necessary and sufficient conditions for its strict convexity. *Journal of International Economics* **3,** 283–290.

Lerner, A. P. (1932). The diagrammatical representation of cost conditions in international trade. *Economica* **12,** 346–356.

Uekawa, Y. (1972). On the existence of incomplete specialization in international trade with capital mobility. *Journal of International Economics* **2,** 1–23.

DEPARTMENT OF ECONOMICS
KOBE UNIVERSITY OF COMMERCE
TARUMI, KOBE
JAPAN

5

On the shape of the single-country and world commodity-substitution and factor-substitution surfaces under conditions of joint production*

MURRAY C. KEMP

RICHARD MANNING

KAZUO NISHIMURA

MAKOTO TAWADA

1. INTRODUCTION

In recent years trade theorists have completed the task of specifying necessary and sufficient conditions for the single-country and world transformation (or production-substitution) surfaces to be locally of any assigned degree of flatness (see Khang and Uekawa, 1973; Kemp *et al.*, 1978; Tawada, 1978). However, those conditions are relevant only if the technology is assumed to be of the no-joint-products type; and trade theorists are showing a growing determination to venture beyond the range of that assumption (see, for example, McKenzie, 1955; Kuga, 1972; Diewert and Woodland, 1977; Woodland, 1977; Chang *et al.*, 1980). Fortunately it is fairly easy to extend the earlier analysis to accommodate jointness of production. Thus, in the present

* We acknowledge with gratitude the very helpful suggestions of Horst Herberg. This chapter first appeared in the *Journal of International Economics*, August 1980.

PRODUCTION SETS   ISBN 0-12-404140-X

chapter, we derive necessary and sufficient conditions for single-country and world production-substitution surfaces to be of any assigned degree of flatness; and we also obtain, as a by-product, necessary and sufficient conditions for single-country and world factor-substitution (or equal-product) surfaces to be of any assigned degree of flatness. Of course, earlier propositions derived from the no-joint-products assumption emerge as special cases. (Some of these cases are noted at the end of Section 2.)

2. A SINGLE COUNTRY

Consider an economy with k industries or sectors, each potentially producing n commodities with the aid of m primary factors of production and of the n produced goods. Let $y^j \equiv (y_1^j, \ldots, y_n^j)'$ be the gross-output vector, $x^j \equiv (x_1^j, \ldots, x_n^j)'$ the intermediate-input vector, and $v^j \equiv (v_1^j, \ldots, v_m^j)'$ the primary-input vector of the jth industry. Then the production possibilities of the jth industry are described by the inequalities[1]

$$(1) \quad f^j(y^j, x^j, v^j) \leqq 0, \quad y^j \geqq 0, \quad x^j \geqq 0, \quad v^j \geqq 0, \quad j = 1, \ldots, k$$

The following restrictions are imposed on f^j.

(A1) f^j is homogeneous of degree one in all of its arguments.

(A2)   If $f^j(\bar{y}^j, \bar{x}^j, \bar{v}^j) \leqq 0$ and $f^j(\bar{\bar{y}}^j, \bar{\bar{x}}^j, \bar{\bar{v}}^j) \leqq 0$, then $f^j(\hat{y}^j, \hat{x}^j, \hat{v}^j) \leqq 0$, where $\hat{y}^j \equiv \theta\bar{y}^j + (1 - \theta)\bar{\bar{y}}^j$, $\hat{x}^j \equiv \theta\bar{x}^j + (1 - \theta)\bar{\bar{x}}^j$, $\hat{v}^j \equiv \theta\bar{v}^j + (1 - \theta)\bar{\bar{v}}^j$, and $\theta \in (0, 1)$.

(A3)   If $(\bar{y}^j, \bar{x}^j, \bar{v}^j)$ and $(\bar{\bar{y}}^j, \bar{\bar{x}}^j, \bar{\bar{v}}^j)$ are not proportional and are such that $f^j(\bar{y}^j, \bar{x}^j, \bar{v}^j) = 0 = f^j(\bar{\bar{y}}^j, \bar{\bar{x}}^j, \bar{\bar{v}}^j)$ then $f^j(\hat{y}^j, \hat{x}^j, \hat{v}^j) < 0$, where $\hat{y}^j \equiv \theta\bar{y}^j + (1 - \theta)\bar{\bar{y}}^j$, $\hat{x}^j \equiv \theta\bar{x}^j + (1 - \theta)\bar{\bar{x}}^j$, $\hat{v}^j \equiv \theta\bar{v}^j + (1 - \theta)\bar{\bar{v}}^j$, and $\theta \in (0, 1)$.

(A4)   If $f^j(y^j, x^j, 0) \leqq 0$, then $y^j = 0$.

(A5)   (i)   If $f^j(\bar{y}^j, x^j, v^j) < 0$, then there exists $\bar{\bar{y}}^j$ such that $\bar{\bar{y}}^j > \bar{y}^j$ and $f^j(\bar{\bar{y}}^j, x^j, v^j) = 0$.

(ii)   If $f^j(\bar{y}^j, x^j, v^j) = 0$, then for any $\bar{\bar{y}}^j$ such that $\bar{\bar{y}}^j \leqq \bar{y}^j$, $f^j(\bar{\bar{y}}^j, x^j, v^j) < 0$.

(iii)   If $f^j(y^j, x^j, \bar{v}^j) < 0$, then there exists $\bar{\bar{v}}^j$ such that $\bar{\bar{v}}^j < \bar{v}^j$ and $f^j(y^j, x^j, \bar{\bar{v}}^j) = 0$.

---

[1] In the statements and proofs of Theorems 1–3 one could suppress intermediate inputs and replace the vector of gross outputs with the vector of net outputs. However, such a streamlined formulation could not readily be extended to allow for the durability of inputs and for nonzero rates of interest. The possibility of such an extension is indicated in the corollary to Theorem 2 and in the concluding remark of Section 3.

(iv)   If $f^j(y^j, x^j, \bar{\bar{v}}^j) = 0$, then for any $\bar{v}^j$ such that $\bar{v}^j \geq \bar{\bar{v}}^j$, $f^j(y^j, x^j, \bar{v}^j) < 0$.

(v)   If $f^j(y^j, \bar{\bar{x}}^j, v^j) = 0$, then for any $\bar{x}^j$ such that $\bar{x}^j \geq \bar{\bar{x}}^j$, $f^j(y^j, \bar{x}^j, v^j) < 0$.

(A2) and (A3) impose suitably generalized quasi concavity on each industry. (A4) states that if no primary factors are available in an industry then it can produce nothing. (A5) is a regularity condition that ensures that all primary factors and all intermediate goods are fully employed. It is slightly stronger than is needed. For example, (A5)(i) and (A5)(iii) could be replaced with the weaker but clumsier assumptions

(A5)(i′)   If $f^j(\bar{y}^j, x^j, v^j) < 0$, then there exists $\bar{\bar{y}}^j$ such that $\bar{\bar{y}}^j \geq \bar{y}^j$, $f^j(\bar{\bar{y}}^j, x^j, v^j) = 0$, and $\sum_{j=1}^k \bar{\bar{y}}^j > \sum_{j=1}^k \bar{y}^j$.

(A5)(iii′)   If $f^j(y^j, x^j, \bar{v}^j) < 0$, then there exists $\bar{\bar{v}}^j$ such that $\bar{\bar{v}}^j \leq \bar{v}^j$, $f^j(y^j, x^j, \bar{\bar{v}}^j) = 0$, and $\sum_{j=1}^k \bar{\bar{v}}^j < \sum_{j=1}^k \bar{v}^j$.

For any given vector $v \equiv (v_1, \ldots, v_m)$ of primary-factor endowments, the set of net production possibilities is

$$(2) \qquad T(v) \equiv \{z \in R^n : f^j(y^j, x^j, v^j) \leq 0, j = 1, \ldots, k, \sum_{j=1}^k y^j = y,$$

$$\sum_{j=1}^k x^j = x, \sum_{j=1}^k v^j \leq v, z \leq y - x\}$$

Notice that the components of the net-output vector z may be of either sign, implying that all commodities can be traded internationally. In view of (A2), $T(v)$ is convex. We consider the problem

$$(M) \qquad\qquad\qquad \max_{z \in T(v)} pz$$

where $p \equiv (p_1, \ldots, p_n) \geq 0$. The solutions of (M), one for each $p \geq 0$, form the production-substitution surface for the given endowment v. The surface is the upper boundary of $T(v)$ and is denoted by $\bar{T}(v)$.

For any given vector $z \equiv (z_1, \ldots, z_n) \equiv y - x$ of net outputs the set of primary-factor requirements is

$$(3) \qquad I(z) \equiv \{v \in R_+^m : f^j(y^j, x^j, v^j) \leq 0, j = 1, \ldots, k, \sum_{j=1}^k y^j = y,$$

$$\sum_{j=1}^k x^j = x, \sum_{j=1}^k v^j \leq v, z \leq y - x\}$$

Again by virtue of (A2), $I(z)$ is convex. We consider the problem

$$(m) \qquad\qquad\qquad \min_{v \in I(z)} wv$$

where $w \equiv (w_1, \ldots, w_m) \geq 0$. The solutions of (m), one for each $w \geq 0$, form the factor-substitution surface for the given net-output vector z. The surface is the lower boundary of $I(z)$ and is denoted by $\bar{I}(z)$.

In defining the production- and factor-substitution surfaces we have not ruled out the possibility that they contain flat faces perpendicular to one or more of the coordinate axes. However, our assumptions (A1)–(A5) do deny such a possibility. We begin our formal analysis by showing that this is so in the case of $\bar{T}(v)$.

LEMMA: Let z^* be in $\bar{T}(v)$ and let $(y^{*j}, x^{*j}, v^{*j}), j = 1, \ldots, k$, be associated with z^*. Then

(a) $f^j(y^{*j}, x^{*j}, v^{*j}) = 0, j = 1, \ldots, k$;
(b)   there are no idle primary factors of production and no idle intermediate goods;
(c) $\bar{T}(v)$ is everywhere negatively sloped.

Proof. (a)   Suppose that, for some j, $f^j(y^{*j}, x^{*j}, v^{*j}) < 0$. Then, from (A5)(i), there exists $\bar{y}^j > y^{*j}$ such that $f(\bar{y}^j, x^{*j}, v^{*j}) = 0$. Hence z^* must lie in the interior of $T(v)$, which is a contradiction.

(b)   Suppose that the ith primary factor is not fully employed at z^*. All or part of the surplus can be assigned to the jth industry, giving it a new vector of primary inputs

$$v^j = (v_1^{*j}, \ldots, v_{i-1}^{*j}, v_i^{*j} + \Delta v_i^j, v_{i+1}^{*j}, \ldots, v_m^{*j})$$

where Δv_i^j is positive. From (A5)(iv),

$$f^j(y^{*j}, x^{*j}, v^j) < 0$$

In view of (A5)(i) there exists a feasible production point $z > z^*$, which is a contradiction.

By a similar argument, relying on (A5)(i) and (A5)(v), there are no idle intermediate goods at z^*.

(c)   It suffices to show that there does not exist $\tilde{z} \in \bar{T}(v)$ such that $\tilde{z} \geq z^*$. Suppose the contrary; and, without loss of generality, let $\tilde{z}_i > z_i^*$. Then in some industries the output of the ith commodity can be reduced by enough to leave total output of that commodity equal to y_i^*. Let

$$\Delta y^j \equiv \tilde{y}^j - y^{*j} = (0, \ldots, \Delta y_i^j, \ldots, 0), \qquad j = 1, \ldots, k$$

Since $z^* \in \bar{T}(v)$,

$$f^j(\tilde{y}^j, \tilde{x}^j, \tilde{v}^j) = 0, \qquad j = 1, \ldots, k$$

Hence, from (A5)(ii),

$$f^j(\bar{y}^j - \Delta y^j, \tilde{x}^j, \tilde{v}^j) < 0 \qquad \text{for some } j$$

That is, z^* is attainable with the factor allocation $(\tilde{x}^j, \tilde{v}^j)$, $j = 1, \ldots, k$, contradicting (a). ∎

Assume now that (A1)–(A5) hold.

THEOREM 1: (i)   Let $\hat{z}$ be any point in the production-substitution surface. Then the surface contains a line segment embracing $\hat{z}$ if and only if there exists a nonzero vector d such that

(a) $Ad = 0$,
(b) $Dd \neq 0$,
(c) $d_j = 0$ if the jth industry is not active, where

$$A \equiv \begin{bmatrix} \hat{v}_1^1 & \cdots & \hat{v}_1^k \\ \vdots & \vdots \\ \hat{v}_m^1 & \cdots & \hat{v}_m^k \end{bmatrix}, \qquad D \equiv \begin{bmatrix} \hat{z}_1^1 & \cdots & \hat{z}_1^k \\ \vdots & \vdots \\ \hat{z}_n^1 & \cdots & \hat{z}_n^k \end{bmatrix}$$

(ii)   Let $\hat{z}$ be any vector of net outputs. Then the factor-substitution surface $\bar{I}(\hat{z})$ contains a line segment if and only if there exists a nonzero vector d^* such that

(a') $Dd^* = 0$,
(b') $Ad^* \neq 0$,
(c') $d_j^* = 0$ if the jth industry is not active.

Proof.   We prove (i) only; (ii) can be proved in a similar manner. Without loss of generality, it is assumed that all k industries are active.

(Necessity)   Suppose that the line segment $(\bar{z}, \bar{\bar{z}})$ lies in $\bar{T}(v)$ and embraces $\hat{z}$. Corresponding to $\bar{z}$ and $\bar{\bar{z}}$ are the points $(\bar{y}^j, \bar{x}^j, \bar{v}^j)$ and $(\bar{\bar{y}}^j, \bar{\bar{x}}^j, \bar{\bar{v}}^j)$, $j = 1, \ldots, k$, which, in view of the lemma, satisfy

$$\sum_{j=1}^{k} \bar{y}^j = \bar{y}, \qquad \sum_{j=1}^{k} \bar{\bar{y}}^j = \bar{\bar{y}}$$

(4)

$$\sum_{j=1}^{k} \bar{x}^j = \bar{x}, \qquad \sum_{j=1}^{k} \bar{\bar{x}}^j = \bar{\bar{x}}$$

$$\sum_{j=1}^{k} \bar{v}^j = \sum_{j=1}^{k} \bar{\bar{v}}^j = \sum_{j=1}^{k} \hat{v}^j = v$$

$$\bar{z} = \bar{y} - \bar{x}, \qquad \bar{\bar{z}} = \bar{\bar{y}} - \bar{\bar{x}}$$

$$f^j(\bar{y}^j, \bar{x}^j, \bar{v}^j) = f^j(\bar{\bar{y}}^j, \bar{\bar{x}}^j, \bar{\bar{v}}^j) = 0$$

Since $\hat{z}$ lies in the line segment $(\bar{z}, \bar{\bar{z}})$, there correspond to $\hat{z}$ the points $(\hat{y}^j, \hat{x}^j, \hat{v}^j)$, $j = 1, \ldots, k$, where, for some $\theta \in (0, 1)$, $\hat{y}^j = \theta\bar{y}^j + (1 - \theta)\bar{\bar{y}}^j$, $\hat{x}^j = \theta\bar{x}^j + (1 - \theta)\bar{\bar{x}}^j$ and $\hat{v}^j = \theta\bar{v}^j + (1 - \theta)\bar{\bar{v}}^j$. From (A2) and the assumption that $\hat{z}$ lies in $\bar{T}(v)$, $f^j(\hat{y}^j, \hat{x}^j, \hat{v}^j) = 0$. Hence, from (A3), there are nonzero λ_j such that

(5) $(\bar{y}^j, \bar{x}^j, \bar{v}^j) = \lambda_j(\bar{\bar{y}}^j, \bar{\bar{x}}^j, \bar{\bar{v}}^j)$, $j = 1, \ldots, k$

From (4), (5), and the definition of $\hat{v}^j$,

$$\sum_{j=1}^{k} \frac{\theta(\lambda_j - 1)}{\theta\lambda_j + 1 - \theta} \hat{v}^j = 0$$

(Since $\bar{z} \neq \bar{\bar{z}}$, not all λ_j are equal to unity.) Defining

$$d_j = \frac{\theta(\lambda_j - 1)}{\theta\lambda_j + 1 - \theta}$$

we then obtain (a) and (c). Finally,

$$\bar{\bar{z}}^j = \frac{1}{\theta\lambda_j + 1 - \theta} \hat{z}^j$$

whence

$$0 \neq \hat{z} - \bar{z} = \sum_{j=1}^{k} (\hat{z}^j - \bar{\bar{z}}^j) = \sum_{j=1}^{k} d_j\hat{z}^j$$

and (b) is obtained.

(Sufficiency)   Suppose that there exists a nonzero vector d satisfying (a)–(c). Given d, we define the new input and output vectors

$$\bar{y}^j = (1 + \alpha d_j)\hat{y}^j, \quad j = 1, \ldots, k$$
$$\bar{v}^j = (1 + \alpha d_j)\hat{v}^j, \quad j = 1, \ldots, k$$
$$\bar{x}^j = (1 + \alpha d_j)\hat{x}^j, \quad j = 1, \ldots, k$$

where the scalar α is chosen so that $1 + \alpha d_j > 0$ for all $j = 1, \ldots, k$. Clearly, from (a),

$$\sum_{j=1}^{k} \bar{v}^j = \sum_{j=1}^{k} \hat{v}^j = v$$

Moreover, from (A1) and the fact that $f^j(\hat{y}^j, \hat{x}^j, \hat{v}^j) = 0$,

$$f^j(\bar{y}^j, \bar{x}^k, \bar{v}^k) = 0$$

Hence

$$\bar{z} \equiv \sum_{j=1}^{k} (\bar{y}^j - \bar{x}^j) \in T(v)$$

Since $\hat{z}$ is in the surface $\overline{T}(v)$, there exists a price vector $p \geq 0$ such that

$$p\hat{z} \geqq p\bar{z} = p \sum_{j=1}^{k} (1 + \alpha d_j)\hat{z}^j = p\hat{z} + \alpha p \sum_{j=1}^{k} d_j\hat{z}^j$$

Since α can have either sign, $p\hat{z} = p\bar{z}$, implying that the line segment is in the surface.

To complete the proof, it must be shown that $\hat{z} \neq \bar{z}$. If $\hat{z} = \bar{z}$, then $\sum_{j=1}^{k} d_j\hat{z}^j = 0$, which contradicts (b). Hence $\hat{z} = \bar{z}$. ■

Our next theorem generalizes Proposition 2 of Kemp *et al.* (1978).

THEOREM 2: (i)   Let $\hat{z}$ be a point in the production-substitution surface. Then the surface contains an r-dimensional flat embracing $\hat{z}$ if and only if at $\hat{z}$ there are exactly r linearly independent vectors in the set

$$S \equiv \{Dd \in R^n : d \text{ satisfies (a) and (c) of Theorem 1}\}$$

(ii)   Let $\hat{v}$ be a point in the factor-substitution surface. Then the surface contains an r-dimensional flat embracing $\hat{v}$ if and only if at $\hat{v}$ there are exactly r linearly independent vectors in the set

$$S^* \equiv \{Ad^* \in R^n : d^* \text{ satisfies (a') and (c') of Theorem 1}\}$$

Proof.   We prove (i) only; (ii) can be proved in a similar manner.

(Sufficiency)   Let there be r vectors $d^1, \ldots, d^r$ such that $Dd^1, \ldots,$ Dd^r are linearly independent. It follows that $Dd^i \neq 0$, $i = 1, \ldots, r$. Corresponding to each d^i we then obtain, by means of the sufficiency part of the proof of Theorem 1, a line segment $(\hat{z}, \bar{z}^i)$ in the product-substitution surface. Since

$$(\hat{z} - \bar{z}^1, \ldots, \hat{z} - \bar{z}^r) = (Dd^1, \ldots, Dd^r)$$

$\hat{z} - \bar{z}^1, \ldots, \hat{z} - \bar{z}^r$ are linearly independent; that is, there exists an r-dimensional flat in the surface and containing $\hat{z}$.

(Necessity)   Suppose that there is an r-dimensional flat in the surface and containing $\hat{z}$. Then we can choose r linearly independent line segments $(\hat{z}, \bar{z}^1), \ldots, (\hat{z}, \bar{z}^r)$, each lying in the surface. In view of the necessity part of the proof of Theorem 1, to any of these segments, say

$(\hat{z}, \bar{z}^i)$, there corresponds a vector d^i satisfying (a)–(c) of Theorem 1; moreover, $\hat{z} - \bar{z}^i = Dd^i$. Hence the set

$$\{Dd \in R^n : d \text{ satisfies (a) and (c) of Theorem 1}\}$$

contains r linearly independent vectors. ∎

Several specializations of Theorem 2(i) are of interest. (α) Let $k = n = m = 2$. If A is singular (that is, if the same factor intensities prevail in both industries), then S contains at most one linearly independent vector and the production substitution surface is locally either linear or strictly concave; thus the familiar result concerning nonjoint production is weakened. If A is nonsingular (that is, if the two industries display different factor intensities), then there are no linearly independent vectors in S and, as in the case of no joint products, the surface is strictly concave. (β) Let $k = n = 3$ and $m = 2$, and let A be of full rank. Then S contains at most one linearly independent vector and locally either the production-substitution surface is a flat of dimension 1 (that is, the surface is ruled, as in the case of no joint products) or it is strictly concave. (γ) Let $k = n \leq m$ and let A be of full rank (so that there are no linearly dependent production processes). Then S contains no linearly independent vectors and locally the production-substitution surface is strictly concave to the origin.

Finally, we offer without proof a corollary to Theorem 2 that relates to the steady states of economies with durable intermediate inputs. It may be compared with Theorem 2 of Kemp *et al.* (1978).

COROLLARY: Suppose that each of the n products may serve as a perfectly durable input to some or all industries, that all m primary factors grow at the common rate g, $g \geq 0$, and that the own-rate of return to any capital good actually produced is equal to g. Suppose also that assumptions (A1)–(A5), suitably reinterpreted, are satisfied. Then Theorem 2, with the production-substitution and factor-substitution surfaces taken in the steady-state sense, continues to hold.

Remark.   One may view the corollary as a generalized "golden-age" or "dynamic" substitution theorem.

3. THE WORLD

Suppose now that there are q countries, with k_v industries in the vth country, $v = 1, \ldots, q$. Each industry in each country potentially produces n commodities with the aid of m primary factors and of the n produced goods. Let $y^{vj} \equiv (y_1^{vj}, \ldots, y_n^{vj})'$ be the gross-output vector, $x^{vj} \equiv (x_1^{vj}, \ldots, x_n^{vj})'$ the intermediate-input vector, and $v^{vj} \equiv (v_1^{vj}, \ldots, v_m^{vj})'$ the primary-input vector of the jth industry in the vth country. Then the production possibilities of the jth industry in the vth country are described by the inequality

$$f^{vj}(y^{vj}, x^{vj}, v^{vj}) \leqq 0, \qquad v = 1, \ldots, q, \quad j = 1, \ldots, k_v$$

Each production function satisfies (A1)–(A5) of Section 2. Every produced commodity is tradable; and the ith primary factor is internationally immobile if $1 \leqq i \leqq m_0$ and otherwise is mobile. The endowment constraints are, therefore,

$$\sum_{j=1}^{k_v} v_i^{vj} \leqq v_i^v, \qquad v = 1, \ldots, q, \quad i = 1, \ldots, m_0$$

$$\sum_{v=1}^{q} \sum_{j=1}^{k_v} v_i^{vj} \leqq v_i, \qquad i = m_0 + 1, \ldots, m$$

where v_i^v is the vth country's endowment of the ith primary factor and $v_i \equiv \sum_{v=1}^{q} v_i^v$. For any given vector $v \equiv (v_1, \ldots, v_m)$ of world primary-factor endowments, the set of net production possibilities is

$$Z(v) \equiv \{ z \in R_+^n : f^{vj}(y^{vj}, x^{vj}, v^{vj}) \leqq 0 \, (v = 1, \ldots, q, j = 1, \ldots, k_v),$$

$$\sum_{v=1}^{q} \sum_{j=1}^{k_v} y^{vj} = y, \; \sum_{v=1}^{q} \sum_{j=1}^{k_v} x^{vj} = x, z \leqq y - x,$$

$$\sum_{j=1}^{k_v} v_i^{vj} \qquad \leqq v_i^v \, (i = 1, \ldots, m_0, v = 1, \ldots, q),$$

$$\sum_{v=1}^{q} \sum_{j=1}^{k_v} v_i^{vj} \leqq v_i \, (i = m_0 + 1, \ldots, m) \}$$

Notice that the components of the net-output vector z are now constrained to be nonnegative (the world is a closed economy). In view of (A2), $Z(v)$ is convex. The world production-substitution surface is the upper boundary $\bar{Z}(v)$ of $Z(v)$.

We can now state and prove the following generalization of Tawada's theorem (Tawada, 1978).

THEOREM 3: Let $\hat{z} \equiv (\hat{z}_1, \ldots, \hat{z}_n) > 0$ be a point in the world production-substitution surface and let an associated factor allocation be described by the matrices

$$A^v \equiv \begin{bmatrix} \hat{v}_1^{v1} & \cdots & \hat{v}_1^{vk_v} \\ \vdots & & \vdots \\ \hat{v}_{m_0}^{v1} & \cdots & \hat{v}_{m_0}^{vk_v} \end{bmatrix}, \qquad v = 1, \ldots, q$$

$$B^v \equiv \begin{bmatrix} \hat{v}_{m_0+1}^{v1} & \cdots & \hat{v}_{m_0+1}^{vk_v} \\ \vdots & & \vdots \\ \hat{v}_m^{v1} & \cdots & \hat{v}_m^{vk_v} \end{bmatrix}, \qquad v = 1, \ldots, q$$

$$D^v \equiv \begin{bmatrix} \hat{z}_1^{v1} & \cdots & \hat{z}_1^{vk_v} \\ \vdots & & \vdots \\ \hat{z}_n^{v1} & \cdots & \hat{z}_n^{vk_v} \end{bmatrix}, \qquad v = 1, \ldots, q$$

Then there exists a nondegenerate line segment that contains $\hat{z}$ and lies in the frontier if and only if there exists a nonzero vector $d \equiv (d_1^1, \ldots, d_{k_1}^1, \ldots, d_1^q, \ldots, d_{k_q}^q)$ such that

(i) $d_j^v = 0$ if the jth industry of the vth country is not active,
(iia) $A^v d^v = 0, v = 1, \ldots, q,$
(iib) $\sum_{v=1}^q B^v d^v = 0,$
(iic) $\sum_{v=1}^q D^v d^v \neq 0,$

where $d^v \equiv (d_1^v, \ldots, d_{k_v}^v)', v = 1, \ldots, q.$

Proof.   Each immobile factor is a vector of q separate factors, each with its own market. Let us therefore define the factor-input matrix

$$A \equiv \begin{bmatrix} A^1 & 0 & \cdots & 0 \\ 0 & A^2 & \cdots & 0 \\ \vdots & \vdots & & \vdots \\ 0 & 0 & \cdots & A^q \\ B^1 & B^2 & \cdots & B^q \end{bmatrix}$$

and the net-output matrix

$$D \equiv \begin{bmatrix} D^1 & D^2 & \cdots & D^q \end{bmatrix}$$

where each column of A and of D is associated with a sector in some country and each row of A is associated with some factor. With these definitions, the proposition follows directly from Theorem 1. ∎

Evidently Theorem 3 reduces to Theorem 1 if $q = 1$.

Theorem 3 tells us nothing about the dimension of any particular flat in the world production-substitution surface. However, by introducing the matrices A and D of the present section into the proof of Theorem 2, it can be shown that the surface contains a ρ-dimensional flat at $\hat{z} > 0$ if and only if the subset

$$\{\textstyle\sum_{v=1}^{q} D^v d^v \in R^n : A^v d^v = 0, v = 1, \ldots, q, \text{ and } \sum_{v=1}^{q} B^v d^v = 0\}$$

contains ρ linearly independent vectors.

Moreover, when suitably reworded, the corollary and Remarks 1 and 3 of Tawada (1978) remain valid when production is joint.

4. AN EXTENSION

Prices do not appear in the statements of Theorems 1–3 and are not essential to the proofs. The theorems therefore can be extended to accommodate constant distortions, whether in the factor markets or the product markets. One need only replace "production-substitution surface" and "factor-substitution surface" with "locus of competitive outputs" and "locus of competitive inputs," respectively.

REFERENCES

Chang, W. W., Ethier, W., and Kemp, M. C. (1980). The theorems of international trade with joint production. *Journal of International Economics* **10**, 377–394.

Diewert, W. E., and Woodland, A. D. (1977). Frank Knight's theorem in linear programming revisited. *Econometrica* **45**, 375–398.

Kemp, M. C., Khang, C., and Uekawa, Y. (1978). On the flatness of the transformation surface. *Journal. of International Economics* **8**, 375–398 (reprinted as Chapter 2 of this volume).

Khang, C., and Uekawa, Y. (1973). The production possibility set in a model allowing interindustry flows: The necessary and sufficient conditions for its strict convexity. *Journal of International Economics* **3**, 283–290.

Kuga, K. (1972). The factor-price equalization theorem. *Econometrica* **40**, 723–736.

McKenzie, L. W. (1955). Equality of factor prices in world trade. *Econometrica* **23**, 239–257.

Tawada, M. (1978). "On the Shape of the World Production Frontier." School of Economics, University of New South Wales (reprinted as Chapter 4 of this volume).

Woodland, A. D. (1977). Joint outputs, intermediate inputs and international trade theory. *International Economic Review* **18**, 517–533.

Murray C. Kemp
SCHOOL OF ECONOMICS
UNIVERSITY OF NEW SOUTH WALES
KENSINGTON, NEW SOUTH WALES
AUSTRALIA

Richard Manning
DEPARTMENT OF ECONOMICS
UNIVERSITY OF CANTERBURY
CHRISTCHURCH, NEW ZEALAND

Kazuo Nishimura
DEPARTMENT OF ECONOMICS
TOKYO METROPOLITAN UNIVERSITY
TOKYO, JAPAN

Makoto Tawada
DEPARTMENT OF ECONOMICS
KOBE UNIVERSITY OF COMMERCE
TARUMI, KOBE
JAPAN

6

Nonsubstitution over the production-possibility frontier

1. INTRODUCTION

Leontief's well-known input–output model is important because it has the potential to show, in a computationally feasible way, the interdependence of the parts of an economy. The model relies on the assumption that inputs to industries must be used in fixed proportions. This contrasts with the view of technical possibilities central to neoclassical economics that inputs may be substituted one for another in an industry without any effect on its output. However, in a remarkable series of papers Arrow (1951), Georgescu-Roegen (1951), Koopmans (1951), and Samuelson (1951) showed that in an economy that allowed input substitution, like the neoclassical world, but in which the economic structure was like that described by Leontief, efficient production required the use of inputs in fixed proportions. That is, even if substitution is possible, there is no need for it to occur in a Leontief system: This is the essence of the nonsubstitution (originally called the substitution) theorem. As a consequence of it, only the fixed coefficients postulated by Leontief could be observed.

There are two, related, types of nonsubstitution theorem. One kind shows that no substitution need take place within an industry as the mixture of outputs is changed along the production-possibility frontier.

51

Copyright © 1982 by Academic Press, Inc.
All rights of reproduction in any form reserved
ISBN 0-12-404140-X

The other kind shows that in a competitive market equilibrium there is a combination of inputs for every industry that is superior to any other technically feasible combination, regardless of the desired composition of final outputs. Proofs of the first type of nonsubstitution theorem frequently, but not always, use concepts of optimization theory (especially of linear programming) that may be interpreted as conditions for competitive equilibria.[1] In this chapter the second type of theorem is explored. This has more intuitive appeal for economists than does the former.

Apart from the intrinsic interest that nonsubstitution has for the Leontief system, the theorem is also of fundamental importance in economics. At the heart of economics is the valuation problem: How are prices determined? The paradigm presented by economists to answer this question is supply and demand analysis. According to this, it is the interaction of demand and supply that determines price. However, in the Leontief system with competitive markets, demand plays no role in price determination: It is costs of production alone that define the (relative) prices of goods. Despite its extension to include the neoclassical feature of substitution, the Leontief model generates a classical result on pricing, stressing costs.[2]

As was quickly noted, the reason for the classical result on pricing is the assumption that there is only one primary resource. This is also critical in establishing the nonsubstitution theorem. That each industry is capable of producing a single product was also noted to be essential for the nonsubstitution theorem. If there are joint products produced by some industries, then the rate of product transformation can vary along the production-possibility frontier, and so the relative prices of produced goods, which are also inputs to industries, vary with outputs. This variation in input prices causes substitution to take place. However, there may be no input substitution within industries as outputs vary over some limited range. Johansen (1972) formalized this idea by developing the concept of nonsubstitution over cones, which he showed held when there were joint products and a single resource.

---

[1] The first type of theorem may be found in Arrow (1951), Chander (1974), Gale (1960), Koopmans (1951), Otani (1973), and Samuelson (1951). Samuelson interpreted his theorem in the second way, however. Theorems of the second type appear in Georgescu-Roegen (1951, Johansen (1972), and Manning (1979, 1981).

[2] Arrow and Starrett (1973) give a full discussion of the classical explanation of price determination and its rival theories.

Work on nonsubstitution has proceeded on the assumption of a single primary resource. Recently, a separate literature has appeared, containing a series of results on the flatness of the production-possibility frontier for economies with neoclassical technologies for the industries and with many primary resources.[3] This generalizes the extended Leontief model, and so permits a generalization of the nonsubstitution theorem to the case with many primary factors. For this case, the concept of nonsubstitution over cones, initiated by Johansen, has been extended by Manning (1981).

In this chapter a nonsubstitution theorem is first presented for the usual case of no joint products and a single primary resource. The proof is novel. The concepts employed are then extended to establish a local nonsubstitution theorem for the general case. These two results establish the connection between competitive equilibria and the flat segments of the production-possibility frontier, along which no substitution of inputs occurs within industries.

To complete the portrait that this chapter gives, the duality of competitive equilibria and efficient input selection is explored. It is shown that in a market economy, the techniques that yield greatest profits also imply the highest real incomes to factor owners. These techniques are the efficient set described by the nonsubstitution theorem.

2. NONSUBSTITUTION WITH ONE PRIMARY RESOURCE AND WITHOUT JOINT PRODUCTS

Consider an economy in which there are n produced goods and a single primary resource. Each produced good is the output of one, and only one, industry. Each industry uses produced goods and the primary resource as inputs. The ith industry has a quasi-strictly concave production function F_i, which exhibits constant returns to scale. Therefore

$$(1) \qquad Y_i \leq F_i(X_{i1}, \ldots, X_{in}, L_i)$$

where Y_i is the gross output of industry i, X_{ij} is the input of commodity j to industry i, and L_i is the input of the primary resource to industry i, $i = 1, \ldots, n$.

---

[3] Khang and Uekawa (1973) and Kemp *et al.* (1978, 1980) show the development of this literature to results of great generality. This work can be viewed as a development of Melvin's celebrated paper (Melvin, 1968) on the two-factor, three-product economy.

Constant returns to scale allow (1) to be written as

(2) $$1 \leq F_i(\alpha_{i1}, \ldots, \alpha_{in}, \beta_i)$$

where $\alpha_{ij} \equiv X_{ij}/Y_i$ and $\beta_i \equiv L_i/Y_i$ are the variable input–output co-efficients for produced good j and the primary resource i in the ith industry. The vector of input–output coefficients will be written (α_i, β_i). The vector (α_i, β_i) is said to be *feasible* if and only if (2) is satisfied by it. It is convenient to define the set of feasible input–output vectors T_i, which will be called the set of techniques available to industry i. In view of the quasi-strict concavity of the production function, T_i is strictly convex.

Commodity j is an output of the jth industry, and an input to all industries. The net output of commodity j is available for consumption. If Z_j is the net output of the jth commodity, then

(3) $$Z_j \leq Y_j - X_{1j} - \cdots - X_{nj}, \qquad j = 1, \ldots, n$$

Given the gross outputs of all industries, and the input–output co-efficients used in them, (3) may be rewritten as

(4) $$Z_j \leq Y_j - \alpha_{1j}Y_1 - \cdots - \alpha_{nj}Y_n, \qquad j = 1, \ldots, n$$

since

(5) $$Y_i \leq \min\left\{\frac{X_{i1}}{\alpha_{i1}}, \ldots, \frac{X_{in}}{\alpha_{in}}, \frac{L_i}{\beta_i}\right\}, \qquad i = 1, \ldots, n$$

All industries use the primary resource, which is in fixed supply L. Total use must not exceed supply, so that

(6) $$L_1 + \cdots + L_n \leq L$$

or, on using (5),

(7) $$\beta_1 Y_1 + \cdots + \beta_n Y_n \leq L$$

Denote by (α, β) the collection of n vectors of input–output co-efficients, one for each industry. If $(\alpha_i, \beta_i) \in T_i$, $i = 1, \ldots, n$, then (α, β) is said to be a *feasible technology*. Given a feasible technology, there is a set of net outputs that the economy is able to produce, namely,

(8) $$\mathbf{Z}(\alpha, \beta) \equiv \{(Z_1, \ldots, Z_n):(4), (7) \text{ are satisfied}; Z_j \geq 0,$$

$$j = 1, \ldots, n; \; Y_i \geq 0, i = 1, \ldots, n\}$$

This is the production-possibility set for a given feasible technology.

In general, a change in the feasible technology will change the production-possibility set associated with it.

The net outputs available to the economy are limited by the availability of the primary resource and what is technically feasible. The *production possibility set* $\mathbf{Z}$ may be defined as follows:

$$(9) \qquad\qquad \mathbf{Z} \equiv \bigcup_{(\alpha,\beta)} \mathbf{Z}(\alpha, \beta)$$

It is easy to prove directly that $\mathbf{Z}$ is convex. What is needed is a more precise characterization of it. In particular, it is important to know whether there is a feasible technology that is superior to all others.

DEFINITION 1:   The economy has the *nonsubstitution property* if and only if there is a feasible technology (α^*, β^*) such that

$$(10) \qquad\qquad \mathbf{Z}(\alpha, \beta) \subseteq \mathbf{Z}(\alpha^*, \beta^*)$$

for all feasible (α, β). (α^*, β^*) is a *dominant technology*.

If (10) holds, then (9) implies that

$$(11) \qquad\qquad \mathbf{Z} = \mathbf{Z}(\alpha^*, \beta^*)$$

That is, the production-possibility set for the economy with substitution possibilities at the level of the industry coincides with the production-possibility set for the economy with input–output coefficients fixed at the dominant values. This occurs because the outputs generated using a dominant technology include the outputs generated in any other way.

Clearly, if there is a dominant technology, then it ought to be adopted. In a perfectly competitive market equilibrium a dominant technology is used. A perfectly competitive equilibrium is defined in a completely standard way, using the constant-returns-to-scale assumption, which implies that no profits are made in equilibrium, so that average revenue (price) equals the average cost of production.

DEFINITION 2:   A *competitive equilibrium* is a positive price for all produced goods and the resource, $p_1^*, \ldots, p_n^*, w^*$, and a feasible technology (α^*, β^*) such that

$$(12) \qquad p_j^* = p_1^* \alpha_{j1}^* + \cdots + p_n^* \alpha_{jn}^* + \beta_j^* w^*, \qquad j = 1, \ldots, n$$

and

$$(13) \qquad p_j^* \leq p_1^* \alpha_{j1} + \cdots + p_n^* \alpha_{jn} + \beta_j w^*, \qquad j = 1, \ldots, n,$$

for all $(\alpha_j, \beta_j) \in T_j$.

In this definition, (12) is the requirement that no profits are made when the equilibrium prices prevail and the equilibrium technology (α^*, β^*) is selected. If any feasible technology other than (α^*, β^*) is selected, then industries' costs would not be lower, so they stand to make losses. A nonsubstitution theorem of the second type is now given.

THEOREM 1: If there is a competitive equilibrium for the economy, then the equilibrium techniques (α^*, β^*) are a dominant technology, and the economy has the nonsubstitution property.

Proof. Suppose otherwise. Then there is a feasible technology (α, β), and a net output Z such that

$$(14) \qquad\qquad Z \geq Z^*$$

where Z^* is any competitive equilibrium output vector.

Now

$$(15) \quad \sum_{j=1}^{n} Z_j p_j^* - Lw^*$$

$$\leq \sum_{j=1}^{n} (-\alpha_{1j} Y_1 - \cdots + (1 - \alpha_{jj}) Y_j - \cdots - \alpha_{nj} Y_n) p_j^*$$

$$- \sum_{j=1}^{n} \beta_j Y_j w^*$$

$$= \sum_{i=1}^{n} (-\alpha_{j1} p_1^* - \cdots + (1 - \alpha_{jj}) p_j^* - \cdots - \alpha_{jn} p_n^* - \beta_j w^*) Y_i$$

$$\leq \sum_{i=1}^{n} (-\alpha_{j1}^* p_1^* - \cdots + (1 - \alpha_{jj}^*) p_j^* - \cdots - \alpha_{jn}^* p_n^* - \beta_j^* w^*) Y_i$$

$$= \sum_{j=1}^{n} (-\alpha_{1j}^* Y_1^* - \cdots + (1 - \alpha_{jj}^*) Y_j^* - \cdots - \alpha_{nj}^* Y_n^*) p_j^*$$

$$- \sum_{j=1}^{n} \beta_j^* Y_j^* w^*$$

$$= \sum_{j=1}^{n} Z_j^* p_j^* - Lw^*$$

The first inequality in (15) is the result of using the definitions of Z_j and L [that is, (4) and (7), respectively]. The first equality holds because the previous expression is rearranged (to allow addition *within* industries to occur before addition across industries). Addition within an industry yields the profits earned. From (12) and (13) the competitive equilibrium techniques generate the maximum profit for all industries. The second inequality follows from this. A rearrangement (to allow addition across industries first) gives the second equality. The final equality holds because positive prices hold only if supply equals demand for all produced goods and the resource.

The first and last terms in (15) imply that

$$(16) \qquad \sum_{j=1}^{n} Z_j p_j^* \leq \sum_{j=1}^{n} Z_j^* p_j^*$$

This contradicts (14), since all $p_j^* > 0$. ∎

The concept of a dominant technology is due to Johansen (1972). The method of proof of this theorem is essentially that used by Manning (1979, Theorem 1), in a different setting, which illustrates one way to extend the nonsubstitution theorem. In a dynamic economy, with durable capital goods, but a single primary resource, there is a best set of techniques, which are identified by the competitive equilibrium.[4] In this case, the average costs of production also include allowances for depreciation and forgone current consumption (time preference). The nonsubstitution theorem then is an alternative way of viewing the well-known "golden rules" of accumulation.

Both the nonsubstitution theorem and results on golden rules determine prices for factors. This suggests that conclusions like nonsubstitution theorems might be found even when universal constant returns to scale are not assumed in models of accumulation. Some very recent calculations indicate that factor proportions are fixed in balanced growth when equilibrium is attained in an economy with some external economies of scale: The essential point is that there is a golden rule for capital accumulation that fixes factor prices. In this case, the production-possibility frontier is nonlinear, and efficient relative prices for outputs need not correspond to the rate of product transformation.[5]

Finally, in connection with this simple economy, note that the supply of the primary resource does not affect the competitive equili-

---

[4] Dynamic nonsubstitution theorems may be found in Burmeister and Dobell (1970), Mirrlees (1969), and Stiglitz (1970).

[5] Such conclusions have been reached by the author and J. R. Markusen in a preliminary draft of a paper.

brium, and so it does not affect the most efficient set of techniques. This observation is of importance in understanding the general case.

3. NONSUBSTITUTION WITH MANY PRIMARY RESOURCES AND WITH JOINT PRODUCTS

Consider now an economy that has n produced goods and r primary resources. There are m producers (or industries). Each producer uses primary resources, and some produced goods, as inputs to generate at least one produced good as an output. In contrast to the case of the previous section, there are many primary factors, not just one, and there are possibly joint products. The latter difference rules out the use of production functions. A set-theoretic approach is used instead.

The ith producer is endowed with a *production set* $\mathbf{T}_i \subseteq R^{n+r}$, $i = 1, \ldots, m$, which is assumed to be a convex cone with vertex 0. There are two parts to this assumption, which correspond to two features of the technology considered in the previous, simpler, case. First, constant returns to scale are allowed when $\mathbf{T}_i$ is a cone with vertex 0. Second, that $\mathbf{T}_i$ is convex implies that there are diminishing rates of substitution between inputs for given outputs (and also diminishing rates of transformation between outputs for given inputs) in an industry. The equivalent property is enjoyed by the isoquants of the quasi-concave production function F_i.

A *feasible production process* is a vector $(a_i, b_i) = (a_{i1}, \ldots, a_{im}, b_{i1}, b_{ir}) \in \mathbf{T}_i$. The convention about $\mathbf{T}_i$ is that $a_{ij} > 0$ if and only if j is produced by i, $a_{ij} < 0$, if and only if j is an input to i, and $a_{ij} = 0$ if and only if j is neither an input nor an output of i. $b_{ij} \geq 0$, with $b_{ij} > 0$ for at least one j.

For ease of comparison with the previous section, it is convenient to normalize the production set, much as input–output coefficients were identified by defining a set related to the unit isoquant in (2). Define T_i in this way:

(17) $T_i \equiv \{(\alpha_i, \beta_i): \exists$ unique scalar $s_i \geq 0$, and for $(a_i, b_i) \in \mathbf{T}_i$,

$$(a_i, b_i) = (\alpha_i, \beta_i)s_i\}$$

T_i is the set of techniques available to producer i. $(\alpha_i, \beta_i) \in T_i$ is a feasible technique. s_i is the scale of production in industry i.

Given the production processes adopted by all producers, net outputs can be computed for all produced goods. In view of the sign conventions on inputs and outputs, for the net output of commodity k

$$(18) \qquad Z_k \le \sum_{i=1}^{m} a_{ik}, \qquad k = 1, \ldots, n$$

The resources used must not exceed the available quantity, so

$$(19) \qquad \sum_{i=1}^{m} b_{ik} \le L_k, \qquad k = 1, \ldots, r$$

where L_k is the fixed supply of resource k.

Alternatively, (18) and (19) may be written as

$$(20) \qquad Z_k \le \sum_{i=1}^{m} \alpha_{ik} s_i, \qquad k = 1, \ldots, n$$

and

$$(21) \qquad \sum_{i=1}^{m} \beta_{ik} s_i \le L_k, \qquad k = 1, \ldots, r$$

Denote by (α, β) the collection of m vectors of techniques, one for each producer. If $(\alpha_i, \beta_i) \in T_i$, $i = 1, \ldots, m$, then (α, β) is said to be a *feasible technology*. Just as (8) does for the case of a single factor and no joint products, so in the general case there can be defined a production-possibility set for a given feasible technology, namely,

$$(22) \qquad \mathbf{Z}(\alpha, \beta) \equiv \{(Z_1, \ldots, Z_n) : (20), (21) \text{ are satisfied}; Z_j \ge 0,$$

$$j = 1, \ldots, n; s_i \ge 0, i = 1, \ldots, m\}$$

The production-possibility set $\mathbf{Z}$ for this economy may be defined in a way analogous to (9) for the simpler case:

$$(23) \qquad \mathbf{Z} \equiv \bigcup_{(\alpha, \beta)} \mathbf{Z}(\alpha, \beta)$$

$\mathbf{Z}$ is convex. However, more can be said about it, if a concept appropriate to express the idea of *local* nonsubstitution over the production-possibility frontier is developed.

At the end of the previous section it was noted that nonsubstitution held not only over the production-possibility frontier but also as the quantity of the primary resource changes (with proportional changes in the outputs of industries). The same must be true in the present general case. If a feasible technology is best for some scales of production and given quantities of resources, then the same technology would also be best if the scales of production and quantities of resources were to be expanded or contracted proportionately. With this understanding, the concept of nonsubstitution over a cone may be developed. $K \subseteq R_+^n$ is a convex cone with vertex 0.

DEFINITION 3: The economy has *nonsubstitution over the cone K* if and only if there is a feasible technology (α^*, β^*) such that

$$(24) \qquad \mathbf{Z}(\alpha, \beta) \cap K \subseteq \mathbf{Z}(\alpha^*, \beta^*) \cap K$$

for all feasible (α, β). (α^*, β^*) is a *dominant technology over the cone K*.

This relates to Definition 1 as follows. If there is a single resource and no joint products, then nonsubstitution holds over all of R_+^n. In this case, there is nonsubstitution over any convex cone with vertex 0 in R_+^n; indeed, the same technology is dominant over every such cone. To appreciate the significance of nonsubstitution in general, therefore, it is important to find the largest cone in which a technology is dominant. This can be done (see Manning, 1981), but is not essential to the present argument.

Dominant technologies ought to be used. They are used in competitive equilibria, which are now defined, again exploiting the fact that no profits will be made because of the assumption of constant returns to scale.

DEFINITION 4: A *competitive equilibrium* is a nonnegative price for all produced goods and resources $p_1^*, \ldots, p_n^*, w_1^*, \ldots, w_r^*$ (not all zero), outputs $Z_1^*, \ldots, Z_n^*$ of produced goods, a technique $(\alpha_i^*, \beta_i^*) \in T_i$, and a scale of production $s_i^* \geq 0$ for producer $i, i = 1, \ldots, m$, such that

$$(25) \qquad \sum_{j=1}^n \alpha_{ij}^* p_j^* - \sum_{j=1}^r \beta_{ij}^* w_j^* = 0, \qquad i \in I^*$$

$$(26) \qquad \sum_{j=1}^n \alpha_{ij} p_j^* - \sum_{j=1}^r \beta_{ij} w_j^* \leq 0 \qquad \text{for all} \quad (\alpha_i, \beta_i) \in T_i, \quad i \in I^*$$

$$(27) \qquad \sum_{j=1}^n \alpha_{ij} p_j^* - \sum_{j=1}^r \beta_{ij} w_j^* < 0 \qquad \text{for all} \quad (\alpha_i, \beta_i) \in T_i, \quad i \notin I^*$$

$$(28) \qquad Z_j^* \leq \sum_{i \in I^*} \alpha_{ij}^* s_i^*, \qquad j = 1, \ldots, n$$

$$(29) \qquad \sum_{i \in I^*} \beta_{ie}^* s_i^* \leq L_e, = \text{only if} \quad e \in E^*, \quad e = 1, \ldots, r$$

(30) $\qquad w_e^* > 0 \qquad$ only if $\ e \in E^*, \quad e = 1, \ldots, r$

(31) $\qquad p_j^* > 0 \qquad$ only if $=$ in (28) for $j, \quad j = 1, \ldots, n$

where I^* is the set of i for which $s_i^* > 0$ and E^* is the set of e such that resource e is fully employed.

This definition is more complicated than Definition 2 to allow for the possibility that in equilibrium some producers may not be in business, some outputs may not be entirely consumed, and some resources may not be fully employed. Each of the bits of the definition is now explained.

I^* identifies those producers who are actually using inputs to produce output. Thus (25) requires that in equilibrium the profit earned by a producer in business be zero. This is analogous to the requirement that price equal the average cost of production in the case without joint products.

Taken with (25), (26) says that maximum profits are zero in equilibrium, since there are no techniques that will bring positive profits.

Any producer not in I^* will make losses in equilibrium if he produces positive outputs, according to (27). These losses can be avoided by not producing. Again maximum profit is zero, this time attained by not producing anything at all.

That the competitive output can be produced by the producers who are in operation is specified by (28), while (31) states that produced goods have positive prices only if they are scarce. This requirement is imposed because with joint products it may happen that producers supply more of one commodity than consumers would buy, even at a zero price. This cannot happen in the absence of joint products. Nor can it happen if consumers are nonsatiated, in the weak sense that for each produced commodity there is at least one consumer who prefers more of it.

Similarly, (29) and (30) limit resource use by the producers to the amount available and state that those resources with positive prices are fully used up. Such a requirement is redundant if there is only one resource. It is also redundant if the excessively strong assumption is made that every primary resource always has a positive marginal productivity in some industry. There is, however, no need for this supposition.

A nonsubstitution theorem of the second type is now given for the case with joint products and many primary resources. This parallels Theorem 1, with the weaker notion of nonsubstitution.

THEOREM 2: If there is a competitive equilibrium for the economy, then the equilibrium technology (α^*, β^*) is dominant over a cone K, and the economy has nonsubstitution over this cone, provided that there is nonsatiation.

Proof. Let there be a cone $K \subseteq R_+^n$ within which the competitive equilibrium prevails. Now suppose, contrary to the theorem, that there is another feasible technology (α, β), and scales of production $s_1, \ldots,$ $s_m \geq 0$, producing the net output vector $Z \in K$, such that

(32) $Z \geq Z^*$

where Z^* is the competitive output vector.

Now

$$
(33) \quad \sum_{k=1}^{n} Z_k p_k^* - \sum_{k=1}^{r} L_k w_k^* \leq \sum_{k=1}^{n} \sum_{i=1}^{m} \alpha_{ik} s_i p_k^* - \sum_{k=1}^{r} \sum_{i=1}^{m} \beta_{ik} s_i w_k^*
$$

$$
= \sum_{i=1}^{m} \left(\sum_{k=1}^{n} \alpha_{ik} p_k^* - \sum_{k=1}^{r} \beta_{ik} w_k^* \right) s_i
$$

$$
\leq \sum_{i \in I^*} \left(\sum_{k=1}^{n} \alpha_{ik}^* p_k^* - \sum_{k=1}^{r} \beta_{ik}^* w_k^* \right) s_i^*
$$

$$
= \sum_{k=1}^{n} \sum_{i \in I^*} \alpha_{ik}^* s_i^* p_k^* - \sum_{k=1}^{r} \sum_{i \in I^*} \beta_{ik}^* s_i^* w_k^*
$$

$$
= \sum_{k=1}^{n} Z_k^* p_k^* - \sum_{k=1}^{r} L_k w_k^*
$$

The first inequality in (33) is the result of using the definitions of Z_k and L_k [that is, (20) and (21), respectively]. The first equality holds because the previous expression is rearranged (to allow addition within industries to occur before addition across industries). Addition within industries yields the profits earned. From (25)–(27) it is known that competitive equilibrium techniques generate the maximum profit for all industries. The second inequality follows from this. A rearrangement gives the second equality. The last equality follows from (28)–(31).

The first and last terms in (33) imply that

$$
(34) \quad \sum_{k=1}^{n} Z_k p_k^* \leq \sum_{k=1}^{n} Z_k^* p_k^*
$$

However, nonsatiation implies that $p_k^* > 0$, for all $k = 1, \ldots, n$. Therefore, (34) contradicts (32). ∎

A comparison of the proofs of Theorems 1 and 2 reveals that they employ the same argument, with a few added complications in the second proof because of the features of joint products and many resources. Theorem 2 is a slightly simplified version of a result presented in Manning (1981). The structure of the cone within which nonsubstitution prevails is spelled out carefully there. One important aspect of this cone is the dimension of its intersection with the production-possibility frontier. A result due to Kemp *et al.* (1980) gives a limit on this dimension, which depends on the ranks of the matrices of the outputs and the inputs.

The generalized nonsubstitution theorem given here may also be extended to dynamic economies and to economies with nonconstant returns to scale.

4. DUALITY

Both (16) and (34) show that the value of output is greatest when competitive equilibrium outputs and methods of production are adopted. This is part of a general duality result, which, in the case without joint products and with a single resource, yields a striking conclusion about prices.

In a market economy, profit is a measure of a producer's ability to pay his way. Firms making losses do not survive. It is possible, however, that firms do not maximize profits, and so they select techniques different from a dominant technology. This motivates the following:

DEFINITION 5: $p_1, \ldots, p_n$ and w are *prices relative to the technology* (α, β) if and only if

$$(35) \qquad p_i \geq p_1\alpha_{i1} + \cdots + p_n\alpha_{in} + w\beta_i, \qquad i = 1, \ldots, n$$

That is, given a feasible technology, selected by firms for whatever reason, the prices for produced goods and the factor are such that firms are able to pay their way. For this given technology the transformation frontier is linear, and the prices are independent of demand.

THEOREM 3: Real competitive equilibrium prices for produced goods are not greater than real prices for produced goods relative to nondominant technologies. That is,

$$(36) \qquad p_i/w \geq p_i^*/w^*, \qquad i = 1, \ldots, n$$

Proof. Without loss of generality, let $w = w^* = 1$. Let Z_j and $Y_j, j = 1, \ldots, n$, satisfy (4) and (7) with equality. Now compute

$$(37) \quad \sum_{j=1}^{n} p_j Z_j - L$$

$$= \sum_{j=1}^{n} \left[-\alpha_{1j} Y_1 - \cdots + (1 - \alpha_{jj}) Y_j - \cdots - \alpha_{nj} Y_n \right] p_j$$

$$\quad - \beta_1 Y_1 - \cdots - \beta_n Y_n$$

$$= \sum_{j=1}^{n} \left[-\alpha_{j1} p_1 - \cdots + (1 - \alpha_{jj}) p_j - \cdots - \alpha_{jn} p_n - \beta_j \right] Y_j$$

$$\geq \sum_{j=1}^{n} \left[-\alpha_{j1}^* p_1^* - \cdots + (1 - \alpha_{jj}^*) p_j^* - \cdots - \alpha_{jn}^* p_n^* - \beta_j^* \right] Y_j$$

$$\geq \sum_{j=1}^{n} \left[-\alpha_{j1} p_1^* - \cdots + (1 - \alpha_{jj}) p_j^* - \cdots - \alpha_{jn} p_n^* - \beta_j \right] Y_j$$

$$= \sum_{j=1}^{n} \left[-\alpha_{1j} Y_1 - \cdots + (1 - \alpha_{jj}) Y_j - \cdots - \alpha_{nj} Y_n \right] p_j^*$$

$$\quad - \beta_1 Y_1 - \cdots - \beta_n Y_n$$

$$= \sum_{j=1}^{n} p_j^* Z_j - L$$

The first equality holds by the definitions of Z_j and L. The second equality is a rearrangement to add within each industry before adding across industries. This gives the total profit earned with prices relative to the technology (α, β). This is nonnegative in view of (35). However, in the competitive equilibrium, profits are zero [see (12)], which establishes the first inequality. The second inequality follows from (12) and (13), which says that profits are maximized in the competitive equilibrium. Rearrangement, and use of the definitions gives the last two equalities.

From the first and last terms of (37),

$$(38) \qquad \sum_{j=1}^{n} p_j Z_j \geq \sum_{j=1}^{n} p_j^* Z_j$$

Consider vectors Z of the form $(0, \ldots, +, \ldots, 0)$; that is, these vectors have zeros everywhere except the jth place. Then (38) implies that

$$p_j \geq p_j^*, \quad j = 1, \ldots, n. \quad \blacksquare$$

This theorem is proved in the same way as is Theorem 2 of Manning (1979) for a dynamic economy. However, the present result is stronger than previous theorems. The concept of an equilibrium relative to a technology originated in Chander (1978), and was used by Manning (1979) in the same form, namely with strict equality in (35). Industries then could not make positive profits in equilibrium. If, however, some industries are distasteful to their managers, in equilibrium positive profits may be earned (negative profits are ruled out since then producers are not paying their way).[6] This consideration admits the stronger definition of prices relative to a technology that is adopted here.

The theorem may be interpreted as proving that deviations from profit maximization by producers will generally lower the real income of resource owners. Certainly, real incomes are not raised. This is a strong result, since it does not depend on any particular pattern of consumption, or on any special properties of consumer preferences.

Taken with (16), (38) when $Z = Z^*$ gives the following result:

$$(39) \qquad \sum_{j=1}^{n} Z_j p_j^* \leq \sum_{j=1}^{n} Z_j^* p_j^* \leq \sum_{j=1}^{n} Z_j^* p_j$$

It was noted at the beginning of this section that the value of output is maximized by competitive equilibrium output: (39) completes the duality by stating that competitive equilibrium prices minimize the value of competitive output.

Definition 5 specifies a weaker kind of equilibrium than does Definition 2. Using the same motivation, a weaker equilibrium for the general case can be defined than Definition 4 in order to find a result like Theorem 3. Such an equilibrium would allow nonnegative profits to those who produce, and losses to other producers unless they avoid production, at the given feasible technology. Then, by proceeding just as in the proof of Theorem 3, it can be shown that

$$(40) \qquad \sum_{j=1}^{n} p_j Z_j - \sum_{j=1}^{r} w_j L_j \geq \sum_{j=1}^{n} p_j^* Z_j - \sum_{j=1}^{r} w_j^* L_j$$

where $p_1, \ldots, p_n, w_1, \ldots, w_r$ are the prices relative to any feasible technology (α, β). In any price system there is a degree of freedom to be used up. This was done in Theorem 3 by taking the price of the

---

[6] For a discussion of such a general equilibrium economy, see Manning (1977).

resource as the *numéraire*. An expression such as (38) is obtained if the prices for the resources are set so that

$$(41) \qquad \sum_{j=1}^{r} w_j L_j = \sum_{j=1}^{r} w_j^* L_j = 1$$

This uses up a degree of freedom in each price system and with (40) implies that

$$(42) \qquad \sum_{j=1}^{n} p_j Z_j \geq \sum_{j=1}^{n} p_j^* Z_j$$

However, the concluding step of the proof of Theorem 3 cannot be taken, since in the present case not all net output vectors are consistent with the *same* competitive equilibrium prices. In a restricted sense it remains true that real income is maximized through profit maximization, as in the case without joint products and with a single resource. The sense here is that the cost of a given bundle of outputs is at the minimum when profits are maximized and total factor income is held constant.

Together, (34) and (42) imply that (39) also holds for the economy with joint products and many resources. This expresses the duality inherent in nonsubstitution in general.

5. CONCLUDING REMARK

This chapter has been concerned with giving a coherent exposition of the major concepts and results involving nonsubstitution theorems. The simple proofs used for the simple, and general, nonsubstitution theorems highlight the nature of the results. Formally, the proofs are like those of the first theorem of welfare economics; the nonsubstitution theorem is essentially a version of that general result.

REFERENCES

Arrow, K. J. (1951). Alternative proof of substitution theorem for Leontief models in the general case. *In* "Activity Analysis of Production and Allocation" (T. C. Koopmans, ed.), pp. 155–164. Wiley, New York.

Arrow, K. J. and Starrett, D. (1973). Cost-and demand-theoretical approaches to the theory of price determination. *In* "Carl Menger and the Austrian School of Economics" (J. R. Hicks and W. Weber, eds.), pp. 129–148. Oxford Univ. Press (Clarendon), London and New York.

Burmeister, E., and Dobell, R. A. (1970). "Mathematical Theories of Economic Growth." Macmillan, New York.

Chander, P. (1974). A simple proof of the non-substitution theorem. *Quarterly Journal of Economics* 88, 698–701.

Chandler, P. (1978). On a planning process due to Taylor. *Econometrica* 46, 761–777.

Gale, D. (1960). "The Theory of Linear Economic Models." McGraw-Hill, New York.

Georgescu-Roegen, N. (1951). Some properties of a generalised Leontief model. *In* "Activity Analysis of Production and Allocation" (T. C. Koopmans, ed.), pp. 165–173. Wiley, New York.

Johansen, L. (1972). Simple and general non-substitution theorems for input-output models. *Journal of Economic Theory* 5, 383–394.

Kemp, M. C., Khang, C., and Uekawa, Y. (1978). On the flatness of the transformation surface. *Journal of International Economics* 8, 537–542 (reprinted as Chapter 2 in this volume).

Kemp, M. C., Manning, R., Nishimura, K., and Tawada, M. (1980). On the shape of the single-country and world commodity substitution and factor substitution surfaces under conditions of joint production. *Journal of International Economics* 10, 395–404 (reprinted as Chapter 5 in this volume).

Khang, C., and Uekawa, Y. (1973). The production possibility set in a model allowing inter-industry flows: The necessary and sufficient conditions for its strict convexity. *Journal of International Economics* 3, 283–290.

Koopmans, T. C. (1951). Alternative proof of the substitution theorem for Leontief models in the case of three industries. *In* "Activity Analysis of Production and Allocation" (T. C. Koopmans, ed.), pp. 147–154. Wiley, New York.

Manning, R. (1977). Some economic consequences of "small-business" behaviour. *Economic Record* 53, 70–82.

Manning, R. (1979). Two theorems concerning optimal educational policy in balanced growth. *Journal of Economic Theory* 21, 465–472.

Manning, R. (1981). A non-substitution theorem with many primary factors. *Journal of Economic Theory* 25, 442–449.

Melvin, J. R. (1968). Production and trade with two factors and three goods. *American Economic Review* 58, 1249–1268.

Mirrlees, J. (1969). The dynamic non-substitution theorem. *Review of Economic Studies* 26, 65–76.

Otani, Y. (1973). Neo-classical technology sets and properties of production possibility sets. *Econometrica* 41, 667–682.

Samuelson, P. A. (1951). Abstract of a theorem concerning substitutability in open Leontief models. *In* "Activity Analysis of Production and Allocation" (T. C. Koopmans, ed.), pp. 142–146. Wiley, New York.

Stiglitz, J. E. (1970). Non-substitution theorems with durable capital goods. *Review of Economic Studies* 27, 543–553.

DEPARTMENT OF ECONOMICS
UNIVERSITY OF CANTERBURY
CHRISTCHURCH, NEW ZEALAND

7

Some implications of variable returns to scale*

HORST HERBERG

MURRAY C. KEMP

1. INTRODUCTION

It is widely believed that the familiar two-dimensional locus of production possibilities becomes uniformly convex to the origin if returns to scale are increasing sufficiently strongly, but remains uniformly concave if returns are only weakly increasing.[1] We shall argue that neither proposition is generally true.

It is also part of received doctrine that when the production-possibility locus is conventionally concave, the output of a commodity in competitive equilibrium increases when its price increases, and that when the locus is convex, equilibrium output responds perversely to an increase in price. It will be argued that in a context of variable returns to scale neither statement is generally valid.

Questions relating to the existence, uniqueness, and stability of competitive international equilibria, as well as many associated

---

* The present paper collates, generalizes, and (therefore) supersedes our earlier separate and partial analyses of the same problems (see Herberg, 1969; Kemp, 1969, Chapter 8) and first appeared in the *Canadian Journal of Economics*, August 1969. The authors acknowledge with gratitude the helpful suggestions of Henry Y. Wan, Jr., and Pham Chi Thanh.
[1] For documentation, see Herberg (1969).

PRODUCTION SETS

ISBN 0-12-404140-X

comparative statical issues, depend for their resolution on the truth or falsity of the propositions advanced above.

In Section 2 our assumptions are laid out; in Sections 3–5 we prove several propositions concerning the simplest case of two factors and two products; and in Section 6 we discuss some possible generalizations.

2. RESTRICTIONS ON PRODUCTION FUNCTIONS AND FACTOR SUPPLIES

A neoclassical technology is assumed, with two final goods produced by two primary factors and no joint products.

Attention is confined to cases in which points on the production possibility locus represent potential competitive equilibria. As is well known, perfect competition and static increasing returns can be reconciled only by the introduction of external economies, and for competitive output to be efficient it suffices that the externalities be output- rather than factor-generated.[2] It will be assumed also that, for the individual firm, returns to scale are constant. The most general individual-firm production functions satisfying these conditions may be written

$$x_j = g_j(X_1, X_2)F_j(v_{j1}, v_{j2}), \qquad j = 1, 2$$

where X_j is the output of the jth industry, x_j is the output of the typical firm in the jth industry, v_{ji} is the typical firm's employment of the ith factor of production, and the "kernel" F_j is homogeneous of the first degree in its arguments. The role of externalities is described by the functions g_j. Thus $\partial g_j/\partial X_i$ tells us the effect on the productivity of a typical firm in the jth industry of a change in the total output of the ith industry. ($\partial g_j/\partial X_i > 0$ for marginal economies, $\partial g_j/\partial X_i < 0$ for diseconomies, and $\partial g_j/\partial X_i = 0$ when externalities are absent.) The industrial production functions, on the other hand, may be written

$$(1) \qquad X_j = g_j(X_1, X_2)F_j(V_{j1}, V_{j2}), \qquad j = 1, 2$$

where V_{ji} is the total employment of the ith factor in the jth industry. Until the final section, however, it will be assumed that, for $i \neq j$, $\partial g_j/\partial X_i = 0$, that is, that scale economies and diseconomies are external to the firm but internal to the industry; until then we shall economize on notation by writing $g_j(X_j)$ instead of $g_j(X_1, X_2)$.

---

[2] The distinction is elaborated in Kemp (1955).

We can now give formal expression of our first assumption.

(A) (i) The output X_j of the jth industry is given by

(2) $$X_j = G_j(V^j) = g_j(X_j)F_j(V^j), \qquad j = 1, 2$$

where $V^j \equiv (V_{j1}, V_{j2})$ is the vector of factor inputs and F_j is a linear homogeneous function defined on R_+^2, the positive quadrant plus the origin. On the positive quadrant F_j possesses continuous second derivatives and positive first derivatives with respect to both arguments, and its isoproduct curves are strictly convex to the origin.

(ii) g_j is a positive function defined on $(0, \infty)$, with a continuous second derivative and an elasticity

(3) $$\omega_j \equiv X_j(dg_j/dX_j)/g_j \equiv X_j g_j'/g_j$$

less than unity.[3]

Clearly $\omega_j > 0$ for locally increasing returns to scale; $\omega_j < 0$ for locally decreasing returns.

The production function defined by (A) is less special than might at first appear. Consider the following alternative to (A).

(A') The output of the jth industry is given by a homothetic production function $X_j = G_j(V^j)$ defined on R_+^2, with continuous second derivatives and positive first derivatives on the positive quadrant and isoproduct curves strictly convex to the origin. Then

THEOREM 1: (A) is satisfied if and only if (A') is satisfied.

Proof. If (A') is satisfied, then there exist two functions F_j and h_j, each determined up to a positive multiplicative factor, such that

(4a) $$Y_j \equiv F_j(V^j) = h_j(G_j(V^j)) = h_j(X_j), \qquad V^j \in R_+^2$$

where F_j satisfies condition (A)(i) and h_j is defined on $(0, \infty)$ with the properties

(4b) $h_j(0) = 0, \qquad h_j' > 0, \qquad h_j''$ continuous for $X_j > 0$

(4c) $\eta_j \equiv (Y_j/h_j^{-1})(dh_j^{-1}/dY_j) > 0 \qquad$ for $Y_j > 0$

Obviously the function g_j defined by

(5) $$g_j = X_j/h_j(X_j), \qquad X_j > 0$$

satisfies (A)(ii). Hence (A) follows from (A').

---

[3] In the uninteresting "explosive" case, with $\omega_j \geqq 1$, we are in the Land of Cockaigne.

Suppose that (A) is satisfied. Then (A$'$) is satisfied, for the required function h_j may be defined by

(6a) $h_j(0) = 0,$ $h_j(X_j) = X_j/g_j(X_j)$ for $X_j > 0$

and

(6b) $\eta_j \equiv 1/(1 - \omega_j)$ for $Y_j > 0.$ ∎

The production functions are subject to two further restrictions:

(B)   As X_j approaches zero the term

$$[1/(1 - \omega_j)^2][(g_j\omega_j/X_j)(1 - \omega_j) + g_j\omega_j']$$
$$= [1/(1 - \omega_j)^2][2g_j'(1 - \omega_j) + X_jg_j'']$$

goes to plus infinity if ω_j is positive, and to minus infinity if ω_j is negative.

(C)   The marginal rates of factor substitution $(\partial F_j/\partial V_{j2})/(\partial F_j/\partial V_{j1})$ have the same range for V^j in the positive quadrant and $j = 1, 2$.

Assumption (B) is not easy to see through. Notice, however, that it is satisfied by production functions G_j that, in a neighborhood of zero output, are homogeneous of constant positive degree $m_j \neq 1$, since then

$$g_j = X_j^{1-n_j}, \qquad \omega_j = 1 - n_j, \quad \text{and} \qquad \omega_j' = 0$$

with $n_j = 1/m_j$. Define $h(X) \equiv X/g(X)$. Then assumption (B) is satisfied also by

$$X = h^{-1}(Y) = Y^k + Y^p$$

for all k and p such that $k \geq p > 0$ with the exception of $k \geq 2$, $p = 1$, and $k = p = 1$. Assumption (C) smooths the argument in Section 3 by ensuring that a certain maximum exists in the positive quadrant. It could be relaxed slightly.[4] Here we note only that (C) holds if (A) holds and if

(C$'$)   The isoproduct curves do not converge to finite points on the coordinate axes.

From (A) and (C$'$) it follows that the range of each marginal rate of substitution is $(0, \infty)$. From (C$'$) it follows that

---

[4] The assumption could be weakened by supposing that (a) the largest set C on which the ratios F_{j2}/F_{j1}, $j = 1, 2$, have the same range is an open, nonempty convex cone in R_+^2 with the origin as vertex and (b) all derivatives F_{ji} and F_{jik} are bounded over C with F_{ji} always greater than some constant positive value.

(C″)   All factors are essential to the production of every good, that is,

$$F_j > 0 \quad \text{implies} \quad V_{ji} > 0, \qquad i, j = 1, 2$$

It should be noted, however, that (C) does not follow from (A) and (C″) only.

If we are to isolate the effect of increasing returns on the shape of the production-possibility locus and on the sensitivity of output to price it is necessary to abstract from changes in factor supplies.

(D)   The total factor supplies $V = (V_1, V_2)$ are positive, finite, and independent of factor and product prices.

3.   THE SHAPE OF THE NEOCLASSICAL LOCUS OF PRODUCTION POSSIBILITIES

Let $\bar{R}_+^2$ stand for the nonnegative quadrant. Then

$$(7) \qquad D^X = \{X \in \bar{R}_+^2 : X_j = G_j(V^j), j = 1, 2, \sum V^j \leqq V\}$$

is the production-possibility set corresponding to the production functions G_1, G_2 and the factor endowment vector V. Similarly,

$$(8) \qquad D^Y = \{Y \in \bar{R}_+^2 : Y_j = F_j(V^j), j = 1, 2, \sum V^j \leqq V\}$$

is the production-possibility set corresponding to the production functions F_1, F_2 and the factor endowment vector V.

The properties of D^Y are easy to establish. Furthermore there exists a continuous one-to-one mapping of D^X onto D^Y defined by

$$(9) \qquad\qquad X_j \leftrightarrow Y_j = h_j(X_j), \qquad j = 1, 2$$

We therefore may hope to establish the shape of D^X by first establishing the shape of D^Y and then, with the aid of the inverse functions h_j^{-1}, examining the "deformation" this set undergoes when it is transformed into D^X.

We begin by proving two lemmas.

LEMMA 1:   Suppose $Y^i \in D^Y$ and $Y_j^i = F_j(V^{ji})$, $i = 0, 1, j = 1, 2$. Let $Y^\alpha = (1 - \alpha)Y^0 + \alpha Y^1$ and $V^{j\alpha} = (1 - \alpha)V^{j0} + \alpha V^{j1}$, $0 < \alpha < 1$. Then $Y_j^\alpha \leqq F_j(V^{j\alpha})$, $j = 1, 2$, with equality if and only if $V^{j0} = \beta_j V^{j1}$ for some positive β_j.

Proof. From the linear homogeneity of F_j,

(10) $$Y_j^\alpha = F_j[(Y_j^\alpha/Y_j^i)V^{ji}], \qquad i = 0, 1$$

Hence the points $Y_j^\alpha V^{j0}/Y_j^0$ and $Y_j^\alpha V^{j1}/Y_j^1$ lie on the same isoproduct curve. By assumption, this curve is strictly convex. Hence

(11) $$Y_j^\alpha \leqq F_j[(1 - \gamma)(Y_j^\alpha/Y_j^0)V^{j0} + \gamma(Y_j^\alpha/Y_j^1)V^{j1}], \quad 0 < \gamma < 1$$

with equality if and only if $V^{j0}/Y_j^0 = V^{j1}/Y_j^1$. On setting $\gamma = \alpha Y_j^1/Y_j^\alpha$ we obtain

(12) $$Y_j^\alpha \leqq F_j(V^{j\alpha}). \quad \blacksquare$$

As an immediate consequence of Lemma 1 we have

LEMMA 2:   The production possibility set D^Y and (trivially) its subset D_1^Y, consisting of all points $Y \in D^Y$ with $Y_1 = 0$, are convex.

Let $\bar{S}^Y$ be the production possibility curve corresponding to the production functions F_1, F_2 and the vector V of factor endowments, and let S^Y be that part of $\bar{S}^Y$ in R_+^2. A point $Y^0 \in R_+^2$ belongs to S^Y if and only if $(0, Y_2^0)$ lies in the interior of D_1^Y and Y_1^0 is the maximum of Y_1 subject to the constraints

(13a) $$H_1 \equiv Y_1 - F_1(V^1) = 0$$

(13b) $$H_2 \equiv Y_2^0 - F_2(V^2) = 0$$

(13c) $$K_i \equiv \sum_j V_{ji} - V_i = 0, \qquad i = 1, 2$$

Introducing the Lagrangian function

(14) $$L \equiv Y_1 - \sum \lambda_j H_j - \sum \mu_i K_i$$

we obtain, as first-order conditions of a maximum, (13) and

(15a) $$\partial L/\partial Y_1 = 1 - \lambda_1 = 0$$

(15b) $$\partial L/\partial V_{ji} = \lambda_j F_{ji} - \mu_i = 0, \qquad i, j = 1, 2$$

where $F_{ji} \equiv \partial F_j/\partial V_{ji}$. It follows that

(16) $$F_{12}/F_{11} = F_{22}/F_{21}$$

Assumption (C) assures us that (16) possesses a solution. Morover, the strict convexity of the isoproduct curves implies that the second-order differential $d^2 L$ is negative for all vectors dY^0 satisfying the restriction $dL = 0$. Hence (16) yields a maximum solution Y_1^0 that is uniquely determined for every Y_2^0 in the interior of D_1^Y. It follows that there exists a well-defined function ψ with the interior of D_1^Y as its domain and such that $Y_1^0 = \psi(Y_2^0)$. S^Y is the graph of ψ. From the definition of S^Y and the convexity of D^Y, ψ is a concave function.

Consider an output vector Y^0 lying on $\bar{S}^Y$. By reasoning similar to that used in the proof of Lemma 1, the inputs V_{ji} $(i, j = 1, 2)$ needed to produce Y^0 are uniquely determined. Thus the V_{ji} are functions f_{ji} of Y^0 with domain $\bar{S}^Y$. From assumption (C) and the fact that the output vector Y^0 requires that all factors be fully employed, the range of the function f_{ji} is a closed interval with positive lower and finite upper bound. Hence the derivatives F_{ji} and $F_{jik} \equiv \partial F_{ji}/\partial V_{jk}$ $(i, j, k = 1, 2)$ are bounded for $Y^0 \in \bar{S}^Y$, with F_{ji} and $-F_{jii}$ being greater than some fixed positive value.

As our next step we show that the first and second derivatives ψ' and ψ'' of ψ are negative and nonpositive, respectively. From (13) and (16) we obtain

$$(17) \qquad \sum_i F_{1i}\, dV_{ji} = \frac{F_{11}}{F_{j1}} \sum_i F_{ji}\, dV_{ji} = (F_{11}/F_{j1})\, dY_j^0$$

$$(18) \qquad \sum_j \sum_i F_{1i}\, dV_{ji} = \sum_i F_{1i} \sum_j dV_{ji} = 0$$

Thus, for all points on S^Y

$$(19) \qquad dY_1^0 = -(F_{11}/F_{21})\, dY_2^0$$

But

$$(20) \qquad dY_1^0 = \psi'\, dY_2^0$$

Hence

$$(21) \qquad \psi' = -F_{11}/F_{21} < 0$$

That

$$(22) \qquad \psi'' \leqq 0$$

follows from the concavity of ψ.

We are now in a position to solve our main problem. Let $\bar{S}^X$ be the locus of production possibilities corresponding to the production functions G_1, G_2 and the vector V of factor endowments, and let S^X be that part of $\bar{S}^X$ in R_+^2. $\bar{S}^X$ is the one-to-one image of $\bar{S}^Y$ under the transformation $X_j^0 = h_j^{-1}(Y_j^0)$, $j = 1, 2$. The function describing S^X

is therefore

(23) $$X_1^0 = \phi(X_2^0) = h_1^{-1}\left[\psi\{h_2(X_2^0)\}\right]$$

Hence, bearing in mind (3) and (5),

(24) $$d\phi = \psi'(h_2'/h_1')\,dX_2^0 = -(F_{11}/F_{21})(h_2'/h_1')\,dX_2^0$$
$$= -(g_1/g_2)(F_{11}/F_{21})\left[(1-\omega_2)/(1-\omega_1)\right]dX_2^0$$

so that

(25) $$dX_1^0/dX_2^0 = -(g_1/g_2)(F_{11}/F_{21})\left[(1-\omega_2)/(1-\omega_1)\right] < 0$$

Moreover,

(26) $$d^2\phi = (1/h_1')\{\psi'' + \left[g_1(\psi')^2/(1-\omega_1)\right]\left[(\omega_1/X_1^0)\right.$$
$$+ (\omega_1'/(1-\omega_1))] - \left[g_2\psi'/(1-\omega_2)\right]\left[(\omega_2/X_2^0)\right.$$
$$+ (\omega_2'/(1-\omega_2))]\}(h_2'\,dX_2^0)^2$$

with

(27) $$\operatorname{sgn} d^2\phi = \operatorname{sgn}\{\ \}$$

since $h_1' > 0$.

In view of assumption (B) and some of our earlier results, $d^2\phi$ is negative for all nonzero dX_2^0 at points $X^0 \in S^X$ with X_1^0 sufficiently close to zero if $\omega_1(X^0)$ is negative there. On the other hand, $d^2\phi$ is positive for all nonzero dX_2^0 at points $X^0 \in S^X$ with X_1^0 sufficiently close to zero if $\omega_1(X_1^0)$ is positive there.

Let $\bar{X}_j$ be the maximum feasible output of the jth good, that is, the X_j-value at which $\bar{S}^X$ reaches the X_j-axis. The term $d^2\phi$ is negative semidefinite at all points of S^X if, for $j = 1, 2$ and $0 < X_j^0 \leq \bar{X}_j$, ω_j is smaller than or equal to zero and ω_j' is always negative or has a sufficiently small positive upper bound. On the other hand, $d^2\phi$ is positive definite everywhere on S^X if, for $j = 1, 2$ and $0 < X_j^0 \leq \bar{X}_j$, ω_j has a sufficiently large positive lower bound and ω_j' has a sufficiently small negative lower bound. In all remaining cases there will normally exist disjoint nonempty parts of S^X where $d^2\phi$ is either indefinite, negative (semi)definite, or positive (semi)definite.[5]

---

[5] The above findings are stated in terms of the differential $d^2\phi$ instead of the derivative ϕ'' since in the present form they can more easily be generalized to the case of n goods and m factors of production.

These and earlier results are pulled together in

THEOREM 2: If assumptions (A)–(D) are satisfied, then the locus of production possibilities $\bar{S}^X$ defined by the production functions G_1, G_2 and the vector of factor endowments V has the following properties:

(a) If for output values near zero the jth good is produced under conditions of decreasing returns to scale [that is, $\lim_{X_j \to 0} \omega_j(X_j) < 0$], then in a neighborhood of zero output of the jth good (but not necessarily at zero output) the locus of production possibilities is strictly concave to the origin, and this is so whatever the nature of scale returns in the other industry. If for output values near zero the jth good is produced under conditions of increasing returns to scale [that is, $\lim_{X_j \to 0} \omega_j(X_j) > 0$], then in a neighborhood of zero output of the jth good (but not necessarily at zero output) the locus of production possibilities is strictly convex to the origin, and this is so whatever the nature of scale returns in the other industry.

(b) The locus of production possibilities is uniformly concave to the origin if, for all feasible outputs, scale returns in each industry (i) are nonincreasing (that is, $\omega_j \leq 0$) and (ii) have not too high positive rates of change with increasing output (that is, ω'_j is negative, or positive but sufficiently small). Condition (i) does not, by itself, ensure concavity.

(c) The production possibility curve is uniformly strictly convex to the origin if, for all feasible outputs, scale returns in each industry (i) are sufficiently strongly increasing (that is, ω_j is positive and sufficiently large) and (ii) have not too low negative rates of change with increasing output (that is, ω'_j is positive, or negative but sufficiently small in magnitude). Condition (i) does not, by itself, ensure strict convexity.

(d) In all other cases the locus of production possibilities may have strictly concave as well as strictly convex parts.

In the interesting but highly special case in which the production functions G_j are homogeneous, so that $G_j = (F_j)^{\eta_j}$, condition (ii) of propositions (b) and (c) is always satisfied, and proposition (d) takes a much stronger form.[6]

---

[6] This case has been considered by Herberg (1969). [Cf also Herberg (1973).]

4. THE RELATION BETWEEN COMMODITY
PRICES AND EQUILIBRIUM OUTPUTS

We seek a parametric representation of outputs in terms of commodity prices. As a means to that end we next set out equations that give expression to the assumptions of competition, full employment, and profit maximization. Let a_{ji} stand for the amount of the ith factor used in the production of a unit of the jth commodity. Then the requirement that both factors be fully employed can be expressed as

$$(28) \qquad \begin{bmatrix} a_{11} & a_{21} \\ a_{12} & a_{22} \end{bmatrix} \begin{bmatrix} X_1 \\ X_2 \end{bmatrix} = \begin{bmatrix} V_1 \\ V_2 \end{bmatrix}$$

Given perfect competition, free entry, and incomplete specialization of production, it follows that in each industry price equals average cost:

$$(29) \qquad \begin{bmatrix} a_{11} & a_{12} \\ a_{21} & a_{22} \end{bmatrix} \begin{bmatrix} w_1 \\ w_2 \end{bmatrix} = \begin{bmatrix} p_1 \\ p_2 \end{bmatrix}$$

where w_i is the price of the ith factor of production, in terms of any *numéraire*, and p_j is the price of the jth product. It remains to give expression to the assumption of profit maximization. By drawing on the first degree homogeneity of F_j, one may write for the production function of a typical producer in the jth industry

$$(30) \qquad 1 = g_j(X_j)F_j(a_{j1}, a_{j2}), \qquad j = 1, 2$$

Let $\chi_j(X_j)$ be the set $\{(a_{j1}, a_{j2})\}$ each member of which satisfies (30):

$$\chi_j(X_j) \equiv \{(a_{j1}, a_{j2}) \in R_+^2 : g_j(X_j)F_j(a_{j1}, a_{j2}) = 1\}$$

Then the problem facing the individual firm is that of minimizing its unit costs:

$$\min_{(a_{j1}, a_{j2}) \in \chi_j(X_j)} w_1 a_{j1} + w_2 a_{j2}$$

As a necessary condition of cost minimization

$$(31) \qquad w_1\, da_{j1} + w_2\, da_{j2} = 0, \qquad j = 1, 2$$

where it is understood that the two increments are consistent with (30).

That completes our specification of the economy. It will prove convenient, however, to place the key equations on a common footing by rewriting (28) and (29) in terms of relative changes of the variables.[7] Differentiating (28) and rearranging slightly, we obtain

$$(32) \qquad \begin{bmatrix} \lambda_{11} & \lambda_{21} \\ \lambda_{12} & \lambda_{22} \end{bmatrix} \begin{bmatrix} \hat{X}_1 \\ \hat{X}_2 \end{bmatrix} = \begin{bmatrix} \hat{V}_1 \\ \hat{V}_2 \end{bmatrix} - \begin{bmatrix} \lambda_{11}\hat{a}_{11} + \lambda_{21}\hat{a}_{21} \\ \lambda_{12}\hat{a}_{12} + \lambda_{22}\hat{a}_{22} \end{bmatrix}$$

where $\lambda_{ji} \equiv V_{ji}/V_i$ is the proportion of the community's endowment of the ith factor employed by the jth industry (so that $\lambda_{1i} + \lambda_{2i} = 1$). In similar fashion, we obtain from (29)

$$(33) \qquad \begin{bmatrix} \theta_{11} & \theta_{12} \\ \theta_{21} & \theta_{22} \end{bmatrix} \begin{bmatrix} \hat{w}_1 \\ \hat{w}_2 \end{bmatrix} = \begin{bmatrix} \hat{p}_1 \\ \hat{p}_2 \end{bmatrix} - \begin{bmatrix} \theta_{11}\hat{a}_{11} + \theta_{12}\hat{a}_{12} \\ \theta_{21}\hat{a}_{21} + \theta_{22}\hat{a}_{22} \end{bmatrix}$$

where θ_{ji} is the share of the ith factor in the costs of the jth industry (so that $\theta_{j1} + \theta_{j2} = 1$). It is easily verified that

$$(33a) \qquad\qquad |\lambda| \equiv \det(\lambda_{ji}) = \lambda_{11} - \lambda_{12}$$

$$(33b) \qquad\qquad |\theta| \equiv \det(\theta_{ji}) = \theta_{11} - \theta_{21}$$

so that the determinants are both positive or both negative as the production of the first or second commodity is relatively intensive in its use of the first factor, and

$$|\lambda| \cdot |\theta| \geq 0$$

Our next step is to eliminate the $\hat{a}_{ij}$ from (32) and (33) with the aid of (31). To convert (31) into the required "circumflex" form is a trivial matter. We must remember, however, that the relative changes in the variables are constrained to satisfy (30) with constant industrial outputs X_j. They are therefore based on *partial* differentials and will be distinguished by a double circumflex:

$$(34) \qquad\qquad \theta_{j1}\hat{\hat{a}}_{j1} + \theta_{j2}\hat{\hat{a}}_{j2} = 0, \qquad j = 1, 2$$

We now introduce, as a convenient shorthand, the elasticity of substitution σ_j for the jth production function. The two elasticities are defined by

$$(35) \qquad\qquad \hat{\hat{a}}_{j1} - \hat{\hat{a}}_{j2} = - \sigma_j(\hat{w}_1 - \hat{w}_2), \qquad j = 1, 2$$

and are assumed to be positive. Again the double circumflex is

---

[7] This notation is borrowed from Jones (1968).

appropriate since the two elasticities are defined in relation to movements around given industrial isoquants. Solving (34) and (35) for the $\mathring{a}_{ji}$, we obtain

$$\mathring{a}_{11} = -\theta_{12}\sigma_1(\hat{w}_1 - \hat{w}_2)$$

$$\mathring{a}_{12} = \theta_{11}\sigma_1(\hat{w}_1 - \hat{w}_2)$$

(36)

$$\mathring{a}_{21} = -\theta_{22}\sigma_2(\hat{w}_1 - \hat{w}_2)$$

$$\mathring{a}_{22} = \theta_{21}\sigma_2(\hat{w}_1 - \hat{w}_2)$$

Finally, we convert the $\mathring{a}_{ji}$ into $\hat{a}_{ji}$ by relaxing the assumption that the X_j are constant and adding to (36) terms that allow for the additional effects of changing X_j. From (2) we infer that $-\omega_j$ is the elasticity of a_{ji} with respect to changes in X_j. Hence our revised equations are

$$\hat{a}_{11} = \mathring{a}_{11} - \omega_1\hat{X}_1 = -\theta_{12}\sigma_1(\hat{w}_1 - \hat{w}_2) - \omega_1\hat{X}_1$$

$$\hat{a}_{12} = \mathring{a}_{12} - \omega_1\hat{X}_1 = \theta_{11}\sigma_1(\hat{w}_1 - \hat{w}_2) - \omega_1\hat{X}_1$$

(37)

$$\hat{a}_{21} = \mathring{a}_{21} - \omega_2\hat{X}_2 = -\theta_{22}\sigma_2(\hat{w}_1 - \hat{w}_2) - \omega_2\hat{X}_2$$

$$\hat{a}_{22} = \mathring{a}_{22} - \omega_2\hat{X}_2 = \theta_{21}\sigma_2(\hat{w}_1 - \hat{w}_2) - \omega_2\hat{X}_2$$

Substituting from (37) into (32) and (33), we obtain

(38)
$$\begin{bmatrix} \lambda_{11} & \lambda_{21} \\ \lambda_{12} & \lambda_{22} \end{bmatrix} \begin{bmatrix} (1 - \omega_1)\hat{X}_1 \\ (1 - \omega_2)\hat{X}_2 \end{bmatrix} = \begin{bmatrix} \hat{V}_1 \\ \hat{V}_2 \end{bmatrix} + (\hat{w}_1 - \hat{w}_2) \begin{bmatrix} \Delta_1 \\ \Delta_2 \end{bmatrix}$$

and

(39)
$$\begin{bmatrix} \theta_{11} & \theta_{12} \\ \theta_{21} & \theta_{22} \end{bmatrix} \begin{bmatrix} \hat{w}_1 \\ \hat{w}_2 \end{bmatrix} = \begin{bmatrix} \hat{p}_1 \\ \hat{p}_2 \end{bmatrix} + \begin{bmatrix} \omega_1\hat{X}_1 \\ \omega_2\hat{X}_2 \end{bmatrix}$$

where $\Delta_1 \equiv \lambda_{11}\theta_{12}\sigma_1 + \lambda_{21}\theta_{22}\sigma_2$ and $\Delta_2 \equiv \lambda_{12}\theta_{11}\sigma_1 + \lambda_{22}\theta_{21}\sigma_2$.

As our last step, we solve (39) for $\hat{w}_1 - \hat{w}_2$ and substitute in (38), then set $\hat{V}_1 = 0 = \hat{V}_2$ and solve for $\hat{X}_1 - \hat{X}_2$:

(40)
$$\hat{X}_1 - \hat{X}_2 = \xi(\omega_1, \omega_2)(\hat{p}_1 - \hat{p}_2)$$

where

(41)
$$\xi(\omega_1, \omega_2) \equiv \left[(1 - \omega_2)\Gamma_1 + (1 - \omega_1)\Gamma_2\right] / \left[(1 - \omega_1)(1 - \omega_2)|\lambda| \cdot |\theta| \right.$$
$$\left. + \omega_1\omega_2(\Delta_1 + \Delta_2) - \omega_1\Gamma_1 - \omega_2\Gamma_2\right]$$

and

(42) $\Gamma_1 \equiv \lambda_{22}\Delta_1 - \lambda_{21}\Delta_2, \qquad \Gamma_2 \equiv \lambda_{12}\Delta_1 - \lambda_{11}\Delta_2$

Equation (40) will be the starting point for all further calculations.

Now let X_j go to zero, so that λ_{ji} goes to zero and, for $k \neq j$, λ_{ki} goes to one. It can be seen that

(43)
$$\lim_{X_j \to 0} \frac{\hat{X}_1 - \hat{X}_2}{\hat{p}_1 - \hat{p}_2} = -\lim_{X_j \to 0} \frac{1}{\omega_j}$$

Thus

THEOREM 3: If in a neighborhood of zero output the jth industry displays increasing returns to scale [that is, $\lim_{X_j \to 0} \omega_j(X_j) > 0$], then the output of the jth good responds perversely to an increase in its relative price, and this is true however weak the tendency to increasing returns in the jth industry and whatever the nature of scale returns in the other industry; if in a neighborhood of zero output the jth industry displays decreasing returns to scale [that is, $\lim_{X_j \to 0} \omega_j(X_j) < 0$], then the output of the jth good responds positively to an increase in its relative price, and this is true however weak the tendency to decreasing returns in the jth industry and whatever the nature of scale returns in the other industry.

It is worth noting that in formula (43) there appears ω_j but not ω_j'. The significance of this will be made clear in Section 5.

Theorem 3 is concerned with the responses of equilibrium outputs near the axes. We now state conditions that, if satisfied, pin down output responses at all points on the curve of production possibilities. We note first, as an implication of assumptions (A) and (C'), that all elasticities of factor substitution have positive lower and finite upper bounds. Since $\omega_j < 1$, it follows that, for X_j in the open interval $(0, \overline{X}_j)$,

$$0 < a_1 \leqq \Delta_i \leqq a_2 < \infty, \qquad i = 1, 2$$
$$0 < \Gamma_i \leqq b_1, \qquad\qquad i = 1, 2$$
$$\Gamma_1 + \Gamma_2 \geqq b_2 > 0$$
$$0 < (1 - \omega_2)\Gamma_1 + (1 - \omega_1)\Gamma_2 \leqq c < \infty$$

where a_i, b_i, and c are constants. We obtain immediately

THEOREM 4: If either $\omega_1 \leqq 0$, $\omega_2 \leqq 0$, $\omega_1 + \omega_2 < 0$, or $\omega_1 \equiv \omega_2 \equiv 0$, $|\lambda| \neq 0$, then $0 < \xi(\omega_1, \omega_2) < \infty$ and the output of each good responds positively to an increase in its relative price; if $\omega_1 \equiv \omega_2 \equiv 0 = |\lambda|$, then $\xi(\omega_1, \omega_2) = \infty$, and if initially production is incompletely specialized, any increase in the price of the jth commodity will result in the complete specialization of production in favour of the jth commodity; if $\omega_i \geqq 0$ and if $\omega_j (j \neq i)$ is sufficiently close to one, then $-\infty < \xi(\omega_1, \omega_2) < 0$ and the output of each good responds perversely to changes in its relative price.

The conditions stated in Theorem 4 are merely sufficient. Thus the output of each commodity may respond positively to an increase in its relative price if ω_j is negative near the boundaries of the interval $(0, \overline{X}_j)$, $j = 1, 2$, but positive everywhere else. However, it does not seem possible to state simple necessary and sufficient conditions for conventional or unconventional output responses without placing severe restrictions on the functions $\omega_1(X_1)$ and $\omega_2(X_2)$.

5. THE RELATION BETWEEN OUTPUT RESPONSES AND THE SHAPE OF THE LOCUS OF PRODUCTION POSSIBILITIES

We have noted in Section 4 that the response of equilibrium outputs to a change in the price ratio depends on ω_j but not on ω_j'. From (26), on the other hand, the local curvature of the locus of production possibilities depends on both ω_j and $\omega_j' (j = 1, 2)$. It is therefore possible to find functions g_j such that

$$\text{sgn}(\hat{X}_1 - \hat{X}_2)/(\hat{p}_1 - \hat{p}_2) \neq \text{sgn}[-(d^2 X_1 / dX_2^2)]$$

Suppose, for example, that $|\lambda| \cdot |\theta| > 0$, $\omega_1 \equiv 0$, and $\omega_2 = 0$ everywhere except in a very tiny interval I near $\overline{X}_2/2$, where it is positive but so small that $\xi(\omega_1, \omega_2)$ remains positive everywhere on S^X. Then it is possible to choose a function $\omega_2(X_2)$ with a derivative ω_2' that is continuous but that increases very sharply to its peak at X_2^* in I and decreases very slowly from there so that, given an arbitrarily large $M > 0$ and an arbitrarily small $N > 0$, $\omega_2' > M$ at some $X_2 = X_2^{**} < X_2^*$ and $-N < \omega_2' \leqq 0$ for all $X_2 > X_2^*$. In particular, it is possible to make M so large that $d^2 X_1 / dX_2^2$ is positive at $X_2 = X_2^{**}$. We have therefore yer (1974a) has cast doubt on the relevance of the earlier findings.[9] ically, he has shown that if a particular dynamic *tâtonnement* alization of the static Herberg–Jones–Kemp model is locally and if several other conditions (inherited from Jones) are satisfied in the context of the static model (a) the Rybczynski conclusions alid, (b) the output of a commodity responds normally to an ase in its price, (c) the Stolper–Samuelson conclusions are valid if oncept of relative factor intensity is reinterpreted in the marginal

this brief comment we offer three observations, the burden of h is that the Herberg–Jones–Kemp perversities cannot be brushed simply on the basis of Mayer's findings.

(i) The confidence with which one can impose stability conditions omparative static calculations is proportional to the confidence one in the realism of one's dynamic extension of the static model. In ducing his dynamic model, Mayer remarks that "[the] assump- s of fixed factor endowments, constant commodity prices, and ect competition virtually prescribe how the dynamic adjustment hanism of the system should be specified." But is this so? In partic- , is one bound by realism to follow Mayer in choosing a *tâtonnement* del? If not, can one be sure that more realistic non-*tâtonnement* dels yield stability conditions that suffice for conclusions (a)–(c)? (ii) Like Stolper, Samuelson, Rybczynski, and Jones, we were ncerned with the comparative static properties of one part of a larger neral-equilibrium system. For purposes of examining those prop- ies it was quite proper to abstract from the rest of the system by ificially freezing commodity prices and factor endowments. How- er, it is not clear that, in searching for stability conditions to impose comparative static calculations within the smaller system, one must ok at a dynamic extension of the *smaller* system. Indeed, there seems be no compelling reason to insist that any particular part of a larger namical system should be stable in isolation.

On the basis of (i) and (ii) we conclude that any attempt (including Iayer's) to dispose of awkward comparative-static results on the basis f stability analysis alone must be viewed as tentative and inconclusive.

[9] In a second paper, Mayer (1974b) has directed a technical criticism at the proof of heorem 2(a) above. However, it has been shown in Herberg and Kemp (1975) that Iayer's criticism is based on a *non sequitur* and, moreover, that the constructive proposi- on of Mayer (1974b) is in fact a special case of Theorem 2(b) above.

THEOREM 5: The response of output to a small price change cannot be inferred from the local curvature of the locus of production possibilities, nor can the latter be inferred from the former.

Theorem 5 will be found paradoxical by anyone who associates competitive equilibria with tangencies of price lines and production-possibility curves. To dispel the paradox it is necessary to observe, first, that when scale returns differ from industry to industry, the price line must *cut* the curve of production possibilities at the equilibrium point; and, second, that when scale returns vary with the level of output, the relation between the price line and the slope of the curve of production possibilities also varies. The first proposition is, perhaps, worthy of formal proof.

For cost minimization by individual firms it is necessary that

$$(44) \qquad (w_2/w_1) = (G_{j2}/G_{j1}) = (F_{j2}/F_{j1}), \qquad j = 1, 2$$

From (15b), interpreting μ_i as w_i, this condition is satisfied for all points of S^Y and, therefore, of S^X. The price ratio is

$$(45) \quad p_2/p_1 = [a_{21} + a_{22}(w_2/w_1)]/[a_{11} + a_{12}(w_2/w_1)] \qquad [\text{from}(29)]$$

$$= (F_{11}/F_{21})(a_{21}F_{21} + a_{22}F_{22})/(a_{11}F_{11} + a_{12}F_{12}) [\text{from}(44)]$$

$$= (g_1/g_2)(F_{11}/F_{21}) \qquad [\text{from the homogeneity of } F_j]$$

Comparing (25) and (45), we arrive at

THEOREM 6: $|dX_1^0/dX_2^0| \gtreqqless p_2/p_1$ at $X^0 \in S^X$ if and only if $\omega_1(X_1^0) \gtreqqless \omega_2(X_2^0)$. Hence, unless $\omega_1 = \omega_2 = $ constant, the price line will intersect the locus of production possibilities except possibly at isolated points.

6. GENERALIZATIONS

Theorems 1–6 relate to the simple world of two primary factors of production and two final products. Moreover, it has been assumed that, while scale economies are external to the firm, they are internal to the industry. Finally, some quite severe restrictions have been placed on both firm and industrial production functions. We now indicate very briefly some of the implications of relaxing earlier assumptions.

That all of our propositions can be rephrased in terms of any number of factors and any number of products will not be found surprising, and our proofs have been set out in a way that lends itself to easy generalization. Here it suffices to state generalizations of Theorems 2 and 6.

THEOREM 2′: If assumptions (A)–(D) are satisfied, the production possibility locus $\bar{S}^X$ defined by the production functions $G_j(V^j) = g_j(X_j)F_j(V^j)$, $V^j = (V_{j1}, \ldots, V_{jm})$, $j = 1, \ldots, n$, and the vector of factor endowments $V = (V_1, \ldots, V_m)$ has the following properties:

(a) If for output values near zero the jth good is produced under conditions of decreasing returns to scale [that is, $\lim_{X_j \to 0} \omega_j(X_j) < 0$] and if each other industry output stands at not less than some positive but otherwise arbitrary level, then in a neighborhood of zero output of the jth good the locus of production possibilities is concave to the origin in every direction, and this is so whatever the nature of scale returns in industries other than the jth. If for output values near zero, the jth good is produced under conditions of increasing returns to scale [that is, $\lim_{X_j \to 0} \omega_j(X_j) > 0$] and if in each other industry output stands at not less than some positive but otherwise arbitrary level, then in a neighborhood of zero output of the jth good the locus of production possibilities is strictly convex to the origin in a least some directions, and this is so whatever the nature of scale returns in industries other than the jth.

(b) The locus of production possibilities is uniformly concave to the origin if, for all feasible outputs, scale returns in each industry (i) are nonincreasing (that is, $\omega_j \leqq 0$) and (ii) have not too high positive rates of change with increasing output (that is, ω_j' is negative or positive but sufficiently small). Condition (i) does not, by itself, ensure concavity.

(c) The locus of production possibilities is uniformly strictly convex to the origin if, for all feasible outputs, scale returns in each industry (i) are sufficiently strongly increasing (that is, ω_j is positive and sufficiently large) and (ii) have not too low negative rates of change with increasing output (that is, ω_j' is positive or negative but sufficiently small in magnitude). Condition (i) does not, by itself, ensure convexity.

(d) In all other cases the locus of production possibilities may have strictly concave as well as strictly convex parts.

THEOREM 6′: $|dX_i^0/dX_j^0| \gtreqless p_j/p_i$ at $X^0 \in S^X$ if and only if $\omega_i(X_i^0) \gtreqless \omega_j(X_j^0)$. Hence unless $\omega_1 = \cdots = \omega_n = $ constant, the price plane will intersect the locus of production possibilities except possibly at isolated points.

Generalizations of a different kind are production functions (1).[8] Consider (4 Section 4. When "cross" externalities are equation is

(46) $\lim_{X_j \to 0} (\hat{X}_1 - \hat{X}_2)/(\hat{p}_1 - \hat{p}_2)$

$$= -\lim_{X_j \to 0} (1 - \omega_{ij} - \omega_{ii})/[\omega_{jj}(1 -$$

where $\omega_{ij} \equiv X_j(\partial g_i/\partial X_j)/g_i$ is the partial el typical firm in the ith industry with respec industry. When $\omega_{ij} = 0$ for $i \neq j$, (46) redu

Finally, the reader is reminded that some on all of assumptions (A)–(D). These assump exist many respectable production funct Consider the following example, which we o

$$X_1 = \min(V_{11}, V_{12}), \qquad X_2 = V_{21}^2$$

Not only is the production possibility locus co of the X_1-axis; it is convex in a neighborhoo

APPENDIX: A REPLY TO THE CRITICI WOLFGANG MAYER

Jones (1968) showed that the Rybczynski ar theorems may break down in the face of variabl we have shown that the output of a commodity m to an increase in its price if returns to scale are

[8] When two industries are technically related, one encou measure of scale returns in either of them separately (or, inc whole). Various conventions suggest themselves. We might ag returns are increasing if an equiproportionate increase in both other industry frozen, results in a more than proportionate in or one might base a definition on a similar calculation with the o held constant; or one might introduce prices and add together th of both industries. Fortunately, calculation need not wait for a

(iii)   In fact, all of Mayer's conclusions require not only stability but also one or more of Jones's three assumptions (1968, pp. 264–267). Thus conclusion (a) relies on Jones's assumption (2), conclusion (b) rests on assumption (3), and conclusion (c) relies on assumption (1). Jones's assumptions are not trivial; nor can we expect that they are implied by stability of the full dynamic model.

REFERENCES

Herberg, H. (1969). On the shape of the transformation curve in the case of homogeneous production functions. *Zeitschrift für die gesamte Staatswissenschaft* **125**, 202–210.

Herberg, H. (1973). On the convexity of the production possibility set under general production conditions. *Zeitschrift für die gesamte Staatswissenschaft* **129**, 205–214.

Herberg, H., and Kemp, M. C. (1975). Homothetic production functions and the shape of the production possibility locus: Comment. *Journal of Economic Theory* **11**, 287–288.

Jones, R. W. (1968). Variable returns to scale in general equilibrium theory. *International Economic Review* **10**, 261–272.

Kemp, M. C. (1955). The efficiency of competition as an allocator of resources. I. External economies of production. *Canadian Journal of Economics and Political Science* **21**, 30–42.

Kemp, M. C. (1969). "The Pure Theory of International Trade and Investment." Prentice-Hall, Englewood Cliffs, New Jersey.

Mayer, W. (1974a). Variable returns to scale in general equilibrium theory: A comment. *International Economic Review* **15**, 225–235.

Mayer, W. (1974b). Homothetic production functions and the shape of the production possibility locus. *Journal of Economic Theory* **8**, 101–110.

Horst Herberg[10]
INSTITUT FÜR INDUSTRIE- UND GEWERBEPOLITIK
UNIVERSITÄT HAMBURG
HAMBURG, WEST GERMANY

Murray C. Kemp
SCHOOL OF ECONOMICS
UNIVERSITY OF NEW SOUTH WALES
KENSINGTON, NEW SOUTH WALES
AUSTRALIA

[10] Present affiliation: Institut für Theoretische Volkswirtschaftslehre, Christian-Albrechts-Universität zu Kiel, Kiel, West Germany.

8

Further implications of variable returns to scale*

HORST HERBERG

MURRAY C. KEMP

MAKOTO TAWADA

1. INTRODUCTION

Several years ago two of the present authors explored some of the implications for the theory of international trade of variable returns to scale in production (Herberg and Kemp, 1969). Of particular interest to the authors of that paper were the properties of the set of production possibilities, the responses of competitive outputs to changes in relative commodity prices, and their interrelations.

The earlier paper contained a special assumption concerning the manner in which the variability of returns is generated. To reconcile increasing returns and perfect competition, and to ensure the coincidence of the production transformation locus and the locus of competitive outputs, it was supposed that returns to scale are constant for the individual firms of an industry but, by virtue of technical intra-industrial externalities, might be increasing or decreasing for the industry as a whole. Specifically, it was assumed that the production function of a typical firm in an industry is the product of a first-degree-homogeneous function of the inputs of the firm and of a positive function of the total output of the industry. It follows from this assumption

* This chapter first appeared in the *Journal of International Economics*, August 1982.

PRODUCTION SETS   ISBN 0-12-404140-X

that the production function of the industry is homothetic. (Of course, for the limited purpose of examining the shape of the production set one need not look behind the industrial production functions; how individual firms enter the picture is irrelevant. But for the purpose of examining price–output responses it is essential to provide a formulation consistent with competitive equilibrium.)

The assumptions of the earlier paper are more or less standard in the recent trade-theoretical literature on variable returns (see, for example, Herberg, 1969; Kemp, 1969, Chapter 8; Melvin, 1969; Kemp and Negishi, 1970; Mayer, 1974a,b; Herberg and Kemp, 1975; Panagariya, 1980). The outstanding exception to the general rule is Jones (1968), who dispensed with the assumption of homotheticity. Nevertheless, not all of those assumptions are plausible, or even necessary to the preservation of perfect competition. In particular, scale effects are supposed to be external to the individual firm generating them but internal to the industry of which the firm is a member. Evidently such an assumption is highly restrictive; for example, it excludes all traditional interindustrial externalities involving air and water pollution.

In the present chapter we provide a more general description of the production side of the economy, allowing the incidence of externalities to lie in any industry and in all industries. We then review some of the implications of variable returns for the topology of the production set, for the sign pattern of price–output responses, and for the traditional Stolper–Samuelson and Rybczynski theorems.[1] As the work of Jones and of Herberg and Kemp (1969) has taught us to expect, propositions with the sweep of standard theorems derived from the assumption of constant returns are no longer available. In particular, conclusions of the Stolper–Samuelson type can be derived only in very special cases. For the rest, however, it is possible to state interesting sufficient conditions for normal or nearly normal responses. In particular, propositions recognizable as close kin to those of standard trade theory can be obtained if interindustrial externalities are nonpositive and, in the case of some propositions, if some mild additional conditions are satisfied. Thus it will be shown that (i) the production transformation locus and the locus of competitive outputs are everywhere negatively sloped, and therefore coincide, if interindustrial externalities are everywhere nonpositive; (ii) the responses of outputs and of the ratio of factor rentals

---

[1] Meade (1952) described the production side of the economy in similar terms, but was interested chiefly in devising a system of taxes to correct for externalities.

to a change in relative commodity prices is everywhere normal if each industry generates nonpositive externalities everywhere, with the interindustrial externalities not stronger than the intraindustrial externalities; and (iii) the responses of outputs to endowment changes are of a weak Rybczynski type (to be defined in Section 6) if the ratio of factor rentals is held constant and if interindustrial externalities are everywhere nonpositive.

Our treatment is not comprehensive. To have aimed at comprehensiveness would have been to undertake the classification of a myriad of special cases. Rather, we have sought an acceptable compromise between such detailed cataloging and a despairing report that anything can happen. However, for those readers who crave a complete catalog, we offer a "do-it-yourself" kit consisting of a set of equations of change involving all endogenous and parametric variables.

2. ASSUMPTIONS AND DEFINITIONS

If allowance is made for the free disposal of outputs, the production possibilities open to the typical firm in the jth industry are described by

(1a) $$z_j^k \leq x_j^k = g^j(X_1, X_2)y_j^k, \qquad j = 1, 2$$

(1b) $$y_j^k = F^j(v_{1j}^k, v_{2j}^k), \qquad j = 1, 2$$

Here v_{ij}^k is the employment of the ith factor of production, x_j^k is the gross or before-disposal output, and z_j^k is the net or after-disposal output, all quantities relating to the typical (kth) firm in the jth industry; uppercase letters indicate industrial quantities, that is, $Z_j := \sum_k z_j^k$, etc. The "kernel" F^j is homogeneous of the first degree in its arguments; hence Y_j is a measure of the level of activity in the jth industry. The role of externalities, on the other hand, is described by the functions g^j of total gross outputs.[2] Thus $g_k^j := \partial g^j / \partial X_k$ describes the impact on the output of a typical firm in the jth industry of a small increase in the level of output of the kth industry. ($g_k^j > 0$ for marginal external economies, $g_k^j < 0$ for marginal external diseconomies, and $g_k^j = 0$ if externalities are absent at the margin.) The weak inequality in (1a) allows for the free disposal of (gross) outputs.

---

[2] Evidently a case could be made for writing g^j as a function of levels of activity instead of levels of output. Such a formulation would retain the link between externalities and inputs, which is a feature of traditional examples of externalities involving air and water pollution.

Industrial production possibilities, on the other hand, are described by

(2a) $$Z_j \leq X_j = g^j(X_1, X_2)Y_j, \qquad j = 1, 2$$

(2b) $$Y_j = F^j(V_{1j}, V_{2j}), \qquad j = 1, 2$$

We now give formal expression to the restrictions imposed on the functions g^j and F^j.

(A1)   The function F^j is defined on the nonnegative quadrant R_+^2, homogeneous of first degree, and strictly quasi-concave. Moreover, in the interior of R_+^2, F^j has positive first- and continuous second-order derivatives. Finally, F^j satisfies the modified Inada conditions

(3a) $$\lim_{V_{1j}/V_{2j} \to 0} F_2^j/F_1^j = 0$$

(3b) $$\lim_{V_{1j}/V_{2j} \to \infty} F_2^j/F_1^j = \infty$$

where $F_i^j := \partial F^j/\partial V_{ij}$.

(A2)   The functions g^j are nonnegative and continuous on R_+^2. Moreover, in the interior of R_+^2, they have continuous derivatives of the first order.

Let us define $X := (X_1, X_2)$, $Y := (Y_1, Y_2)$, and

(4) $$G^j(X) := X_j/g^j(X), \qquad G(X) := (G^1(X), G^2(X))$$

(A3) $Y = G(X)$ is a globally univalent mapping (bijection) from R_+^2 onto R_+^2 with

(i) G and G^{-1} continuous,
(ii) $G^j = 0$ if and only if $X_j = 0$, and
(iii) $\lim_{X_k \to 0} G_k^j$ finite, $j \neq k$, for any given positive X_j.

Let us further define

(5) $$\epsilon_{jk} := X_k g_k^j/g^j$$

the elasticity of the output of the jth commodity with respect to the output of the kth commodity.

Now $G_k^j = -\epsilon_{jk} G^j/X_k$. Hence G_k^j remains finite as X_k goes to zero only if at the same time ϵ_{jk} goes to zero, $j \neq k$. Thus (A3) implies that

(6) $$\lim_{X_k \to 0} \epsilon_{jk} = 0, \qquad j \neq k, \qquad \text{for any given positive } X_j$$

and rules out the possibility that an industry is subject to strong external effects generated by the other industry when the later is operating at a low level.

To rule out the Land of Cockaigne and to ensure univalence of the mapping (4), it is assumed that the Gale–Nikaido conditions for univalence,

(A4) $1 - \epsilon_{jj} > 0,$ $j = 1, 2$

$$\Delta := (1 - \epsilon_{11})(1 - \epsilon_{22}) - \epsilon_{12}\epsilon_{21} > 0$$

are satisfied.

Finally, without loss of generality, it is assumed that

(A5) the first industry is relatively intensive in its use of the first factor of production.

EXAMPLE: Let

(7a) $g^j(X) = X_j^{\epsilon_{jj}}(1 + X_k)^{\delta_j},$ $j, k = 1, 2,$ $j \neq k$

where ϵ_{jj} and δ_j are constants and such that

(7b) $1 - \epsilon_{jj} > 0,$ $(1 - \epsilon_{11})(1 - \epsilon_{22}) - \delta_1\delta_2 > 0$

Noticing that

(7c) $\epsilon_{jk} = \delta_j X_k/(1 + X_k),$ $j \neq k$

it is easy to verify that (A2)–(A4) are satisfied.

Let V_i be the (positive) endowment of the ith factor of production, $i = 1, 2$. Then the set of Y-production possibilities is

$$S_Y := \{Y : Y_j = F^j(V_{1j}, V_{2j}), j = 1, 2; \sum_{j=1}^{2} V_{1j} \leq V_i, i = 1, 2\}$$

and the Y-production transformation locus is the upper boundary $\bar{S}_Y^u$ of S_Y, that is,[3]

$$\bar{S}_Y^u := \{Y : Y \in S_Y \text{ and } \nexists Y' \in S_Y \text{ with } Y' \geq Y\}$$

As is well known, S_Y is convex and $\bar{S}_Y^u$ negatively sloped and strictly convex from above. Moreover, $\bar{S}_Y^u$ is the locus of all Y-output points

[3] As usual, $Y' \geqq Y$ means $Y'_j \geqq Y_j, j = 1, 2$; $Y' \geq Y$ means $Y' \geqq Y$ but $Y' \neq Y$; and $Y' > Y$ means $Y'_j > Y_j, j = 1, 2$.

associated with efficient production; that is,

$$\bar{S}_Y^u = \bar{S}_Y^e := \{ Y : Y \in S_Y \text{ and } \nexists Y' \in S_Y \text{ with } Y' > Y \}$$

It will be convenient to describe $\bar{S}_Y^u = \bar{S}_Y^e$ by the function

(8) $$Y_1 = \psi(Y_2) \qquad (\psi' < 0, \psi'' < 0)$$

Similarly, the set of Z-production possibilities is

$$S_Z := \{ Z : 0 \leqq Z_j \leqq X_j = g^j(X)F^j(V_{1j}, V_{2j}), j = 1, 2;$$

$$\sum_{j=1}^{2} V_{ij} \leqq V_i, i = 1, 2 \}$$

$$= \{ Z : 0 \leqq Z \leqq X = G^{-1}(Y), Y \in S_Y \}$$

The Z-production transformation locus $\bar{S}_Z^u$ and the set of efficient Z-production points $\bar{S}_Z^e$ are defined analogously to $\bar{S}_Y^u$ and $\bar{S}_Y^e$. Since outputs are assumed to be freely disposable, $\bar{S}_Z^u$ has nonpositive slope everywhere. Moreover, the negatively sloped part of $\bar{S}_Z^u$, if it is not empty, coincides with $\bar{S}_Z^e$. The locus $\bar{S}_Z^e$ is never empty but may consist of a single point.

3. THE PRODUCTION TRANSFORMATION LOCUS AND THE LOCUS OF COMPETITIVE OUTPUTS

In the absence of all externalities, the set S_Z of production possibilities is convex and the production transformation locus $\bar{S}_Z^u$ negatively sloped. Under the special assumptions of Herberg and Kemp (1969), $\bar{S}_Z^u$ remains negatively sloped, but S_Z is no longer necessarily convex. Under the more general assumptions of the present chapter, not even negativity of slope can be taken for granted. In the present section we show by example that the slope need not be everywhere negative and then provide a sufficient condition for negativity of slope.

LEMMA 1: Efficient output points Z or X are associated with output points Y obtained under conditions of full employment and efficient allocation of factors; hence such points can be attained under conditions of perfect competition.

Proof. Let us define

$$S_X := G^{-1}(S_Y), \qquad \Sigma_X := G^{-1}(\bar{S}_Y^u)$$

Thus S_X is the set of production possibilities without free disposal and Σ_X is the locus of competitive outputs. Since G^{-1} is a continuous bijection, it maps the boundary $\bar{S}_Y$ of S_Y onto the boundary $\bar{S}_X$ of S_X:

$$\bar{S}_X = G^{-1}(\bar{S}_Y)$$

The same property of G^{-1} implies that S_X, as the image of the compact set S_Y, is also compact and hence contains a nonempty subset $\bar{S}_X^e$ of efficient output points. Moreover, for every $Z \in S_Z$ there exists $X \in S_X$ and $X^e \in \bar{S}_X^e$ such that $Z \leq X \leq X^e$. Hence (i) S_Z is compact and (ii) $\bar{S}_Z^e$, the set of efficient output points in S_Z, is nonempty and coincides with $\bar{S}_X^e$. Finally, we observe that, by virtue of (A3)(ii), $X_j = 0$ if and only if $Y_j = 0$. Bearing in mind that $\bar{S}_Z^e$ and $\bar{S}_X^e$ belong to the upper boundary of their respective sets, both are subsets of Σ_X, the locus of competitive outputs. ∎

Like $\bar{S}_Z^e$, $\bar{S}_X^e$ either consists of a single point or is downward-sloping everywhere; more specifically, $\bar{S}_X^e$ is the downward-sloping part of the locus of competitive outputs Σ_X.

We can now provide the promised example in which Σ_X and therefore $\bar{S}_Z^u$ are not everywhere of negative slope and in which, therefore, $\bar{S}_X^e$ and $\bar{S}_Z^e (= \bar{S}_X^e)$ are proper subsets of Σ_X and $\bar{S}_Z^u$, respectively. Let X belong to $\Sigma_X = G^{-1}(\bar{S}_Y^u)$. From (2a),

(9) $$Y_j = X_j/g^j(X) = G^j(X), \qquad j = 1, 2$$

Moreover, Y belongs to $\bar{S}_Y^u$. Hence

$$X_1 = g^1(X)\psi(G^2(X))$$

Defining

(10) $$\phi(X) := X_1 - g^1(X)\psi(G^2(X))$$

we obtain

(11) $$dX_2/dX_1 = -\phi_1/\phi_2$$

where

(12a) $$\phi_1 = 1 - g_1^1\psi - g^1\psi'G_1^2 = (1 - \epsilon_{11}) - g^1\psi'G_1^2$$

(12b) $$\phi_2 = -(g_2^1\psi + g^1\psi'G_2^2)$$

and $\phi_j := \partial\phi/\partial X_j$. From the definition of G^2 [Eq. (4)],

(13a) $$G_1^2 = -X_2 g_1^2/(g^2)^2$$

(13b) $$G_2^2 = (1 - \epsilon_{22})/g^2 > 0$$

EXAMPLE: Let us return to the special g^j functions (7). Substituting from (13) into (12) and then from (12) into (11), and bearing in mind (7), we find that

(14a)
$$\frac{dX_2}{dX_1} = \frac{(1 - \epsilon_{11}) + g^1 g_1^2 X_2 \psi'/(g^2)^2}{g_2^1 \psi + g^1(1 - \epsilon_{22})\psi'/g^2}$$

that is,

(14b)

$$\frac{dX_2}{dX_1} = \frac{(1 - \epsilon_{11}) + \delta_2 X_1^{\epsilon_{11}} X_2^{1 - \epsilon_{22}}(1 + X_1)^{-1-\delta_2}(1 + X_2)^{\delta_1}\psi'}{\delta_1 X_1(1 + X_2)^{-1} + X_1^{\epsilon_{11}} X_2^{-\epsilon_{22}}(1 + X_1)^{-\delta_2}(1 + X_2)^{\delta_1}(1 - \epsilon_{22})\psi'}$$

Let δ_2 be positive and ϵ_{11} negative. Then, for sufficiently small X_1, both numerator and denominator must have the sign of ψ', which is negative. For sufficiently small X_1, therefore, dX_2/dX_1 is positive, and dZ_2/dZ_1 equals zero. Figure 1 provides an illustration.

Thus the assumptions made so far must be strengthened if $\bar{S}_Z^u$ is to be necessarily of negative slope everywhere.

PROPOSITION 1: Given assumptions (A1) and (A4), a sufficient but not necessary condition for the production transformation locus $\bar{S}_Z^u$ and the locus of competitive outputs Σ_X to be everywhere downward

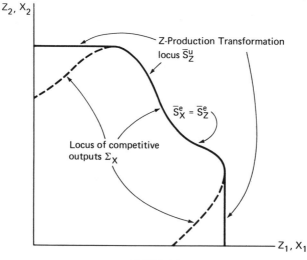

FIGURE 1

sloping and hence to coincide is that both interindustrial externalities be nonpositive throughout ($\epsilon_{12} \leqq 0$, $\epsilon_{21} \leqq 0$).

Proof.   Rewriting (14a) as

$$dX_2/dX_1 = \frac{(1 - \epsilon_{11}) + (g^1 X_2/g^2 X_1)\psi' \epsilon_{21}}{(X_1/X_2)\epsilon_{12} + (g^1/g^2)\psi'(1 - \epsilon_{22})}$$

the conclusion follows by inspection.   ■

Remark Concerning Proposition 1.   The condition of Proposition 1 reappears in most of our remaining propositions, including all propositions of global applicability. Those propositions therefore relate indifferently to points on the production transformation locus and to points on the locus of competitive outputs.

We could go on to consider the curvature of the production transformation locus. However, we already know from the earlier work of Herberg and Kemp (1969) that, even in the absence of interindustrial externalities, nonconstant returns to scale may cause the locus to be entirely convex, entirely concave, or to have convex as well as concave parts, and that in general the curvature is unrelated to the price–output response. Thus the added complication of interindustrial externalities cannot be expected to generate new results of more than passing interest. For the little that can be gleaned in this field, the reader is referred to Tawada (1980).

Similarly, we could examine the relation between the price ratio and the slope of the locus of competitive outputs. But it is known, again from the work of Herberg and Kemp (1969), that the relative slopes of the price line and of Σ_X convey almost no information about price–output responses or other matters treated in the present chapter. We simply note, without proof, that, unless $\epsilon_{11} \equiv \epsilon_{22} \equiv$ const. and $\epsilon_{21} \equiv \epsilon_{12} \equiv 0$, Σ_X is cut by the price line except possibly at isolated points.

4.   PRICES, OUTPUTS, AND RELATIVE FACTOR REWARDS

We now examine the relation between commodity prices, on the one hand, and competitive outputs and relative factor rentals, on the other. Of course, all output points to be considered must lie on the locus of competitive outputs. They may or may not lie on the production transformation locus; if they lie on an upward-sloping stretch of the locus of competitive outputs, then they cannot also lie on the production transformation locus.

To the familiar production relations

(15) $X_j = g^j(X_1, X_2)F^j(V_{1j}, V_{2j}), \qquad j = 1, 2$

and the full-employment equalities

(16) $\sum_{j=1}^{2} V_{ij} = V_i, \qquad i = 1, 2$

we now add the zero-profit condition of competitive equilibrium,

(17) $\sum_{i=1}^{2} w_i V_{ij} = p_j X_j, \qquad j = 1, 2$

where p_j is the price of the jth commodity and w_i is the rental of the ith factor of production. Differentiating (15), and noticing that, under competition,

$$w_i = p_j g^j(X_1, X_2)F_i^j, \qquad i, j = 1, 2$$

we obtain

(18) $\begin{bmatrix} 1 - \epsilon_{11} & -\epsilon_{12} \\ -\epsilon_{21} & 1 - \epsilon_{22} \end{bmatrix} \begin{bmatrix} \hat{X}_1 \\ \hat{X}_2 \end{bmatrix} = \begin{bmatrix} \theta_{11}\hat{V}_{11} + \theta_{21}\hat{V}_{21} \\ \theta_{12}\hat{V}_{12} + \theta_{22}\hat{V}_{22} \end{bmatrix}$

where $\theta_{ij} := w_i V_{ij}/p_j X_j$ is the share of the ith factor in the cost of producing the jth commodity. And, differentiating (16), we obtain

(19) $\begin{aligned} \lambda_{11}\hat{V}_{11} + \lambda_{12}\hat{V}_{12} &= \hat{V}_1 \\ \lambda_{21}\hat{V}_{21} + \lambda_{22}\hat{V}_{22} &= \hat{V}_2 \end{aligned}$

where $\lambda_{ij} := V_{ij}/V_i$ is the proportion of the ith factor allocated to the jth industry. Finally, differentiating (17) gives

(20) $\begin{bmatrix} \theta_{11} & \theta_{21} \\ \theta_{12} & \theta_{22} \end{bmatrix} \begin{bmatrix} \hat{w}_1 \\ \hat{w}_2 \end{bmatrix} = \begin{bmatrix} \hat{X}_1 + \hat{p}_1 - (\theta_{11}\hat{V}_{11} + \theta_{21}\hat{V}_{21}) \\ \hat{X}_2 + \hat{p}_2 - (\theta_{12}\hat{V}_{12} + \theta_{22}\hat{V}_{22}) \end{bmatrix}$

As is well known,

(21) $\begin{aligned} |\theta| &= \theta_{11}\theta_{22} - \theta_{12}\theta_{21} = \theta_{11} - \theta_{12} = \theta_{22} - \theta_{21} \\ |\lambda| &= \lambda_{11}\lambda_{22} - \lambda_{12}\lambda_{21} = \lambda_{11} - \lambda_{21} = \lambda_{22} - \lambda_{12} \end{aligned}$

so that, in view of (A5),

(22) $|\theta| > 0, \qquad |\lambda| > 0$

From (18) and (20),

$$(23) \qquad \begin{bmatrix} \theta_{11} & \theta_{21} \\ \theta_{12} & \theta_{22} \end{bmatrix} \begin{bmatrix} \hat{w}_1 \\ \hat{w}_2 \end{bmatrix} = \begin{bmatrix} \hat{p}_1 + \epsilon_{11}\hat{X}_1 + \epsilon_{12}\hat{X}_2 \\ \hat{p}_2 + \epsilon_{21}\hat{X}_1 + \epsilon_{22}\hat{X}_2 \end{bmatrix}$$

We next define the (positive) elasticity of factor substitution σ_j by the relation

$$(24) \qquad \hat{V}_{2j} - \hat{V}_{1j} = \sigma_j(\hat{w}_1 - \hat{w}_2) = \sigma_j\hat{\omega}$$

where $\omega := w_1/w_2$. Equations (19) and (24) can then be solved for $\hat{V}_{1j}$ and $\hat{V}_{2j}$:

$$(25a) \qquad \hat{V}_{11} = \frac{1}{|\lambda|}[\lambda_{22}\hat{V}_1 - \lambda_{12}\hat{V}_2 + \lambda_{12}(\lambda_{21}\sigma_1 + \lambda_{22}\sigma_2)\hat{\omega}]$$

$$(25b) \qquad \hat{V}_{12} = \frac{-1}{|\lambda|}[\lambda_{21}\hat{V}_1 - \lambda_{11}\hat{V}_2 + \lambda_{11}(\lambda_{21}\sigma_1 + \lambda_{22}\sigma_2)\hat{\omega}]$$

$$(25c) \qquad \hat{V}_{21} = \frac{1}{|\lambda|}[\lambda_{22}\hat{V}_1 - \lambda_{12}\hat{V}_2 + \lambda_{22}(\lambda_{11}\sigma_1 + \lambda_{12}\sigma_2)\hat{\omega}]$$

$$(25d) \qquad \hat{V}_{22} = \frac{-1}{|\lambda|}[\lambda_{21}\hat{V}_1 - \lambda_{11}\hat{V}_2 + \lambda_{21}(\lambda_{11}\sigma_1 + \lambda_{12}\sigma_2)\hat{\omega}]$$

The solutions are independent of outputs, and therefore of the ϵ, because they describe movements along the Y-contract locus. Finally, inserting (25) into (18) and defining

$$(26a) \qquad \Delta_1 := \lambda_{11}\theta_{21}\sigma_1 + \lambda_{12}\theta_{22}\sigma_2 > 0$$

$$(26b) \qquad \Delta_2 := \lambda_{21}\theta_{11}\sigma_1 + \lambda_{22}\theta_{12}\sigma_2 > 0$$

and

$$(27a) \qquad \mu_1 := \lambda_{21}\Delta_1 + \lambda_{11}\Delta_2$$

$$(27b) \qquad \mu_2 := \lambda_{22}\Delta_1 + \lambda_{12}\Delta_2$$

we obtain

$$(28a) \qquad \begin{bmatrix} 1 - \epsilon_{11} & -\epsilon_{12} \\ -\epsilon_{21} & 1 - \epsilon_{22} \end{bmatrix} \begin{bmatrix} \hat{X}_1 \\ \hat{X}_2 \end{bmatrix} = \frac{1}{|\lambda|} \begin{bmatrix} (\lambda_{22}\hat{V}_1 - \lambda_{12}\hat{V}_2 + \mu_2\hat{\omega}) \\ -(\lambda_{21}\hat{V}_1 - \lambda_{11}\hat{V}_2 + \mu_1\hat{\omega}) \end{bmatrix}$$

or, equivalently,

(28b)
$$
\begin{bmatrix} (1 - \epsilon_{11})\lambda_{11} - \epsilon_{21}\lambda_{12} & (1 - \epsilon_{22})\lambda_{12} - \epsilon_{12}\lambda_{11} \\ (1 - \epsilon_{11})\lambda_{21} - \epsilon_{21}\lambda_{22} & (1 - \epsilon_{22})\lambda_{22} - \epsilon_{12}\lambda_{21} \end{bmatrix} \begin{bmatrix} \hat{X}_1 \\ \hat{X}_2 \end{bmatrix}
$$
$$
=: \begin{bmatrix} \lambda'_{11} & \lambda'_{12} \\ \lambda'_{21} & \lambda'_{22} \end{bmatrix} \begin{bmatrix} \hat{X}_1 \\ \hat{X}_2 \end{bmatrix} = \begin{bmatrix} \hat{V}_1 + \Delta_1\hat{\omega} \\ \hat{V}_2 - \Delta_2\hat{\omega} \end{bmatrix}
$$

It can be easily verified that

(29)
$$ |\lambda'| = \Delta|\lambda| > 0 $$

Equations (23) and (28) are the starting point of all further calculations.
  Solving (28) gives

(30)
$$
\begin{bmatrix} \hat{X}_1 \\ \hat{X}_2 \end{bmatrix} = \frac{1}{|\lambda'|} \begin{bmatrix} \lambda'_{22}\hat{V}_1 - \lambda'_{12}\hat{V}_2 + \eta_2\hat{\omega} \\ \lambda'_{21}\hat{V}_1 - \lambda'_{11}\hat{V}_2 - \eta_1\hat{\omega} \end{bmatrix}
$$

where

(31)
$$
\begin{aligned}
\eta_1 &:= (1 - \epsilon_{11})\mu_1 - \epsilon_{21}\mu_2 = \lambda'_{21}\Delta_1 + \lambda'_{11}\Delta_2 \\
\eta_2 &:= -\epsilon_{12}\mu_1 + (1 - \epsilon_{22})\mu_2 = \lambda'_{22}\Delta_1 + \lambda'_{12}\Delta_2
\end{aligned}
$$

Substituting from (30) into (23) yields

(32)
$$
\begin{bmatrix} \theta_{11} - \xi_1 & \theta_{21} + \xi_1 \\ \theta_{12} - \xi_2 & \theta_{22} + \xi_2 \end{bmatrix} \begin{bmatrix} \hat{w}_1 \\ \hat{w}_2 \end{bmatrix}
$$
$$
=: \begin{bmatrix} \theta'_{11} & \theta'_{21} \\ \theta'_{12} & \theta'_{22} \end{bmatrix} \begin{bmatrix} \hat{w}_1 \\ \hat{w}_2 \end{bmatrix} = \begin{bmatrix} \hat{p}_1 + \rho_{12}\hat{V}_1 - \rho_{11}\hat{V}_2 \\ \hat{p}_2 + \rho_{22}\hat{V}_1 - \rho_{21}\hat{V}_2 \end{bmatrix}
$$

with

(33a)
$$ \rho_{ji} := \frac{1}{|\lambda'|}(\epsilon_{j1}\lambda'_{i2} - \epsilon_{j2}\lambda'_{i1}), \qquad i, j = 1, 2 $$

(33b)
$$ \xi_j := \frac{1}{|\lambda'|}(\epsilon_{j1}\eta_2 - \epsilon_{j2}\eta_1), \qquad j = 1, 2 $$

Since $\theta'_{1j} + \theta'_{2j} = 1$, we have $|\theta'| = \theta'_{11} - \theta'_{12} = \theta'_{22} - \theta'_{21}$ and

(34)
$$ |\theta'| = |\theta| + \xi_2 - \xi_1 $$

From (32) we see at once that, in general, w_1, w_2, and ω depend not
only on p_1 and p_2 but also on V_1 and V_2 and that, therefore, factor
rentals will not be equated across countries even when specialization
is incomplete and the same techniques of production are available

everywhere. Thus, solving (32),

$$(35) \qquad \hat{\omega} = - \frac{1}{|\theta'|} \left[\hat{p} + (\rho_{22} - \rho_{12})\hat{V}_1 - (\rho_{21} - \rho_{11})\hat{V}_2 \right]$$

$$= - \frac{1}{|\theta'|^*} \left[|\lambda'|\hat{p} + (\rho_{22}^* - \rho_{12}^*)\hat{V}_1 - (\rho_{21}^* - \rho_{11}^*)\hat{V}_2 \right]$$

where

$$(36a) \qquad p := p_2/p_1$$

$$(36b) \qquad \rho_{ji}^* := |\lambda'| \rho_{ji}$$

$$(36c) \qquad \xi_j^* := |\lambda'| \xi_j$$

$$(36d) \qquad |\theta'|^* := |\lambda'| \cdot |\theta'| = \Delta|\lambda| \cdot |\theta| + \xi_2^* - \xi_1^*$$

From (28a) and (35), with $\hat{V}_i = 0$, $i = 1, 2$,

$$(37a) \qquad \hat{X}_1 = - \frac{\eta_2}{|\theta'|^*} \hat{p}$$

$$(37b) \qquad \hat{X}_2 = \frac{\eta_1}{|\theta'|^*} \hat{p}$$

and

$$(38) \qquad \hat{\omega} = - \frac{|\lambda'|}{|\theta'|^*} \hat{p}$$

Thus the sign of $|\theta'|$ is critical in determining the direction of response of outputs and relative factor rentals. Under (A5) all responses are normal if $|\theta'|^*$ is positive, abnormal if $|\theta'|^*$ is negative. The sign of $|\theta'|^*$ depends in turn on the sign of $\xi_2^* - \xi_1^*$. Now

$$(39a) \qquad \xi_2^* - \xi_1^* = (\epsilon_{21} - \epsilon_{11})\eta_2 + (\epsilon_{12} - \epsilon_{22})\eta_1$$

that is,

$$(39b) \qquad \xi_2^* - \xi_1^* = \left[\epsilon_{21}(1 - \epsilon_{12}) - \epsilon_{11}(1 - \epsilon_{22}) \right]\mu_2$$
$$+ \left[\epsilon_{12}(1 - \epsilon_{21}) - \epsilon_{22}(1 - \epsilon_{11}) \right]\mu_1$$

In general, $\xi_2^* - \xi_1^*$ may be of either sign. However, it is possible to find simple restrictions on the ϵ_{jk} that ensure normal responses. We begin with a global proposition.

PROPOSITION 2: The responses of outputs and of the ratio of factor rentals to a change in relative commodity prices is everywhere normal if $\epsilon_{11} \leqq \epsilon_{21} \leqq 0$ and $\epsilon_{22} \leqq \epsilon_{12} \leqq 0$.

Proof. It must be shown that $|\theta'|^*$ is positive. Suppose that the condition is satisfied. Then, from (31), both η_1 and η_2 are positive; hence, by virtue of (39a), $\xi_2^* - \xi_1^* \geqq 0$; hence, from (36d), $|\theta'|^*$ is positive. ∎

Our next proposition is local in scope. From (21), as the economy moves to complete specialization in either commodity, $|\lambda|$, and therefore $|\lambda'|$, goes to zero; thus, as λ_{11} goes to zero or as λ_{12} goes to zero, the sign of $|\theta'|^*$ depends on the sign of $\xi_2^* - \xi_1^*$. Let us denote by ϵ_{jk}^1 the limit of ϵ_{jk} as λ_{11} goes to zero and by ϵ_{jk}^2 the limit of ϵ_{jk} as λ_{12} goes to zero. Then, recalling (6),

(40a) as $\lambda_{11} \to 0$: $\quad \mu_1 \to 0, \quad \mu_2 \to \sigma_2 > 0,$

$$\eta_1 \to 0, \quad \eta_2 \to (1 - \epsilon_{22}^1)\sigma_2 > 0$$

$$\xi_2^* - \xi_1^* \to -\epsilon_{11}^1(1 - \epsilon_{22}^1)\sigma_2 \neq 0 \qquad \text{if} \quad \epsilon_{11}^1 \neq 0$$

(40b) as $\lambda_{12} \to 0$: $\quad \mu_1 \to \sigma_1 > 0, \quad \mu_2 \to 0,$

$$\eta_1 \to (1 - \epsilon_{22}^2)\sigma_1 > 0, \quad \eta_2 \to 0$$

$$\xi_2^* - \xi_1^* \to -\epsilon_{22}^2(1 - \epsilon_{11}^2)\sigma_1 \neq 0 \qquad \text{if} \quad \epsilon_{22}^2 \neq 0$$

Applying (40) to (37), we obtain

PROPOSITION 3: If X_j is sufficiently small, then the ratio of factor rentals and the output of the jth industry respond normally or abnormally to changes in commodity prices according as the jth industry is subject to diminishing or increasing returns. If X_j is sufficiently small and if the kth industry is subject to nonpositive interindustrial externalities ($\epsilon_{kj} \leqq 0$, $k \neq j$), then the output of the kth industry ($k \neq j$) responds normally or abnormally to changes in commodity prices according as the jth industry is subject to diminishing or increasing returns. These conclusions are independent both of the returns to scale in and of the externalities received by the other industry.[4,5]

---

[4] The last two propositions are special cases (for $\epsilon_{jk} \equiv 0$, $j \neq k$) of results reported in Herberg and Kemp (1969), Theorems 3 and 4.

[5] For sufficiently strong positive interindustrial externalities ϵ_{kj}, $k \neq j$, however, η_j may be negative at small enough X_j. Under such circumstances, the output response to commodity price changes will be normal in one industry and abnormal in the other industry. (It will be recalled that the same condition is necessary for the locus of competitive outputs to be positively sloped for sufficiently small X_j.)

5.   THE STOLPER–SAMUELSON THEOREM

In Section 4 we studied the response of relative factor rentals to changes in commodity prices. We now turn our attention to the individual rentals.

From (32),

$$(41a) \qquad \hat{w}_1 - \hat{p}_j = -\frac{\theta'_{2j}}{|\theta'|}\hat{p} = -\frac{\theta^*_{2j}}{|\theta'|^*}\hat{p}, \qquad j = 1, 2$$

$$(41b) \qquad \hat{w}_2 - \hat{p}_j = \frac{\theta'_{1j}}{|\theta'|}\hat{p} = \frac{\theta^*_{1j}}{|\theta'|^*}\hat{p}, \qquad j = 1, 2$$

where

$$(42) \qquad\qquad \theta^*_{ij} := |\lambda'|\theta'_{ij}$$

Thus the Stolper–Samuelson conclusion is valid if $|\theta'|^*$ and all θ^*_{1j} are positive. We notice at once that this condition cannot be met near the axes. For there $|\theta'|^*$ may be negative; moreover, θ^*_{1j} and θ^*_{2j} tend to be of opposite sign.

Let us try to be more precise. We shall say that the Stolper–Samuelson conclusions hold in their weak form if $(\hat{w}_1 - \hat{p}_j)/\hat{p} < 0$ and $(\hat{w}_2 - \hat{p}_j)/\hat{p} > 0, j = 1, 2$. We have

$$(43a) \qquad \left. \begin{aligned} \lim \xi^*_1 &= -\lim|\theta'|^* = \lim \theta^*_{21} \\ &= -\lim \theta^*_{11} = \epsilon^1_{11}(1 - \epsilon^1_{22})\sigma_2 \\ \lim \xi^*_2 &= \lim \theta^*_{22} = \lim \theta^*_{12} = 0 \\ \lim(\hat{w}_1 - \hat{p}_1)/\hat{p} &= \lim(\hat{w}_2 - \hat{p}_1)/\hat{p} = 1 \\ &\qquad\qquad\quad \text{if} \quad \epsilon^1_{11} \neq 0 \end{aligned} \right\} \quad \text{as} \quad \lambda_{11} \to 0$$

$$(43b) \qquad \left. \begin{aligned} \lim \xi^*_1 &= \lim \theta^*_{21} = \lim \theta^*_{11} = 0 \\ \lim \xi^*_2 &= \lim|\theta'|^* = \lim \theta^*_{22} \\ &= -\lim \theta^*_{12} = -\epsilon^2_{22}(1 - \epsilon^2_{11})\sigma_1 \\ \lim(\hat{w}_1 - \hat{p}_2)/\hat{p} &= \lim(\hat{w}_2 - \hat{p}_2)/\hat{p} = -1 \\ &\qquad\qquad\quad \text{if} \quad \epsilon^2_{22} \neq 0 \end{aligned} \right\} \quad \text{as} \quad \lambda_{12} \to 0$$

Moreover,

$$(44a) \qquad \text{if } \lambda_{11} \text{ is small enough, if } \epsilon^1_{11} \neq 0,$$

$$\text{and if } \epsilon_{12} \leqq 0, \epsilon_{21} \leqq 0, \epsilon_{22} > 0, \text{ then}$$

$$\text{sgn}(\hat{w}_2 - \hat{p}_2)/\hat{p} = \text{sgn}(-\epsilon^1_{11})$$

and

(44b)   if λ_{12} is small enough, if $\epsilon_{22}^2 \neq 0$,

and if $\epsilon_{12} \leqq 0$, $\epsilon_{21} \leqq 0$, $\epsilon_{11} > 0$, then

$$\text{sgn}(\hat{w}_1 - \hat{p}_1)/\hat{p} = \text{sgn}(-\epsilon_{22}^2)$$

Thus we have verified

PROPOSITION 4: If X_j is sufficiently small and subject to non-constant returns to scale, then an increase in the relative price of the jth commodity gives rise to a decline in both factor rentals in terms of the jth commodity. This is so independently of the returns to scale in the other industry and of the sign of any inter-industrial externalities. Moreover, for small X_j, real rentals in terms of the other commodity may change in either direction, depending in part on the nature of interindustrial externalities.

Thus, even in their weak form, the Stolper–Samuelson conclusions cease to hold under variable returns to scale and interindustrial externalities.

We conclude this section with a brief remark concerning the number of switches of response. Suppose that ϵ_{11}^1 is positive. If $|\theta'|^*$ and θ_{11}^* are positive somewhere then, as the first industry shrinks, they must change sign at least once, for both are negative for sufficiently small λ_{11}. Since the changes of sign are unlikely to occur at the same output point, we can expect $(\hat{w}_2 - \hat{p}_1)/\hat{p}$ to change sign at least twice, from plus to minus to plus. However, θ_{21}^* may be positive everywhere; hence there is at least one change in the sign of $(\hat{w}_1 - \hat{p}_1)/\hat{p}$, from minus to plus.

6. THE RYBCZYNSKI THEOREM

From (23) we see that, under variable returns to scale, factor rentals may change when factor endowments change even if commodity prices are held constant; and that commodity prices may change when endowments change even if factor rentals are held constant. Thus, under variable returns, we cannot hold constant both commodity prices and factor rentals while we examine the response of outputs to changes in endowments. Accordingly, the analysis of this section falls into two parts, first proceeding on the assumption that $\hat{\omega} = 0$, then on the assumption that $\hat{p} = 0$. Conformably, we distinguish between an ω-version of the Rybczynski theorem and a p-version.

A second distinction will be useful. We shall say that weak Rybczynski conclusions hold if

(45)
$$\hat{X}_j/\hat{V}_i > 0, \qquad i, j = 1, 2, \quad i = j$$
$$\hat{X}_j/\hat{V}_i < 0, \qquad i, j = 1, 2, \quad i \neq j$$

and we shall say that strong Rybczynski conclusions hold if

(46)
$$\hat{X}_j/\hat{V}_i > 1, \qquad i, j = 1, 2, \quad i = j$$
$$\hat{X}_j/\hat{V}_i < 0, \qquad i, j = 1, 2, \quad i \neq j$$

Case 1: $\hat{\omega} = 0$. In this case factor intensities do not change and it is possible to establish a global generalization of the Rybczynski theorem.

PROPOSITION 5: (a) If the interindustrial externalities are non-positive ($\epsilon_{12} \leqq 0, \epsilon_{21} \leqq 0$), then weak Rybczynski conclusions are valid everywhere, whatever the returns to scale in each industry.

(b) If in addition returns to scale are nondecreasing in each industry ($\epsilon_{jj} \geqq 0, \; j = 1, \; 2$), then strong Rybczynski conclusions are valid everywhere.

Proof. (a) Bearing in mind that $|\lambda'| > 0$ and that if $\epsilon_{12} \leqq 0$ and $\epsilon_{21} \leqq 0$, then $\lambda'_{ij} > 0$, the conclusion follows by inspection of (28b).

(b) From (28b), (29), and the definition of Δ,

$$(47) \quad \lambda'_{22} - |\lambda'| = (1 - \epsilon_{22})\lambda_{22} - \epsilon_{12}\lambda_{21} - \Delta(\lambda_{22} - \lambda_{12})$$
$$= [\epsilon_{11}(1 - \epsilon_{22}) + \epsilon_{12}\epsilon_{21}]\lambda_{22} - \epsilon_{12}\lambda_{21} + \Delta\lambda_{12}$$
$$> 0 \quad \text{if} \quad \epsilon_{11} \geqq 0, \quad \epsilon_{12} \leqq 0, \quad \epsilon_{21} \leqq 0$$

Similarly,

$$(48) \quad \lambda'_{11} - |\lambda'| > 0 \quad \text{if} \quad \epsilon_{22} \geqq 0, \quad \epsilon_{12} \leqq 0, \quad \epsilon_{21} \leqq 0 \quad \blacksquare$$

In addition, the following local proposition is available:

PROPOSITION 6: For sufficiently small X_1, $\hat{X}_1/\hat{V}_1 > 1$ and $\hat{X}_1/\hat{V}_2 < -1$: and for sufficiently small X_2, $\hat{X}_2/\hat{V}_2 > 1$ and $\hat{X}_1/\hat{V}_2 < -1$. These conclusions are independent of returns to scale and of the sign of interindustrial externalities.

Proof. The conclusion follows from (28b) and the fact that, as λ_{ij} goes to 1, $\lambda'_{ij} - |\lambda'|$ goes to $1 - \epsilon^k_{jj} > 0, j \neq k$. $\blacksquare$

Remark. In some intermediate range of the output locus, with λ_{ij} sufficiently different both from 0 and from 1, it is possible that $\hat{X}_1/\hat{V}_1 < 0$ and $\hat{X}_1/\hat{V}_2 > 0$ if $\epsilon_{12} > 0$, and that $\hat{X}_2/\hat{V}_1 > 0$ and $\hat{X}_2/\hat{V}_2 < 0$ if $\epsilon_{21} > 0$. Thus, if interindustrial externalities are positive, then even the weak Rybczynski conclusions may not hold. For global versions of the Rybczynski theorem, the nature of interindustrial externalities is decisive.

Case 2: $\hat{p} = 0$. Again we have one proposition of global applicability and one of local applicability. As might have been expected, however, the propositions are even more fragmentary than in case 1.

PROPOSITION 7: (a)   If $\epsilon_{11} \leq \epsilon_{21} \leq 0$ and $\epsilon_{22} \leq \epsilon_{12} \leq 0$, then the output responses to endowment changes are everywhere normal in the restricted sense that $\hat{X}_1/\hat{V}_1 > 0$ and $\hat{X}_2/\hat{V}_2 > 0$.

(b) If $\epsilon_{21} \leq \min(0, \epsilon_{11})$ and $\epsilon_{12} \leq \min(0, \epsilon_{22})$, then $\hat{X}_1/\hat{V}_2$ and $\hat{X}_2/\hat{V}_1$ are either both negative or both positive, according as the response of factor rentals to commodity price changes is normal or abnormal.[6]

Proof. (a)   From (35), with $\hat{p} = 0$,

(49) $$\hat{\omega} = \frac{1}{|\theta'|^*}\left[(\rho_{12}^* - \rho_{22}^*)\hat{V}_1 - (\rho_{11}^* - \rho_{21}^*)\hat{V}_2\right]$$

Substituting from (49) into (30) gives

(50a) $$\hat{X}_1 = \frac{1}{|\lambda'\|\theta'|^*}\{[\lambda_{22}'|\theta'|^* + \eta_2(\rho_{12}^* - \rho_{22}^*)]\hat{V}_1$$
$$- [\lambda_{12}'|\theta'|^* + \eta_2(\rho_{11}^* - \rho_{21}^*)]\hat{V}_2\}$$

(50b) $$\hat{X}_2 = -\frac{1}{|\lambda'\|\theta'|^*}\{[\lambda_{21}'|\theta'|^* + \eta_1(\rho_{12}^* - \rho_{22}^*)]\hat{V}_1$$
$$- [\lambda_{11}'|\theta'|^* + \eta_1(\rho_{11}^* - \rho_{21}^*)]\hat{V}_2\}$$

Now from (33a) and (36b)

(51) $$\rho_{1j}^* - \rho_{2j}^* = (\epsilon_{11} - \epsilon_{21})\lambda_{j2}' + (\epsilon_{22} - \epsilon_{12})\lambda_{j1}'$$

Hence, bearing in mind (38b), the terms on the right-hand side of (50)

---

[6] Both for (a) and (b) the other output changes are generally indeterminate.

can be transformed as follows. Taking the first term of (50a), we obtain

(52a)
$$|\theta'|^* \lambda'_{22} + \eta_2(\rho^*_{12} - \rho^*_{22})$$
$$= |\lambda'\|\theta|\lambda'_{22} + (\epsilon_{12} - \epsilon_{22})(\lambda'_{22}\eta_1 - \lambda'_{21}\eta_2)$$
$$= |\lambda'\|\theta|\lambda'_{22} + (\epsilon_{12} - \epsilon_{22})\Delta(\lambda_{22}\mu_1 - \lambda_{21}\mu_2)$$
$$= |\lambda'|[|\theta|\lambda'_{22} + (\epsilon_{12} - \epsilon_{22})\Delta_2]$$

Similarly,

(52b) $\quad |\theta'|^* \lambda'_{12} + \eta_2(\rho^*_{11} - \rho^*_{21}) = |\lambda'|[|\theta|\lambda'_{12} - (\epsilon_{12} - \epsilon_{22})\Delta_1]$

(52c) $\quad |\theta'|^* \lambda'_{21} + \eta_1(\rho^*_{12} - \rho^*_{22}) = |\lambda'|[|\theta|\lambda'_{21} - (\epsilon_{21} - \epsilon_{11})\Delta_2]$

(52d) $\quad |\theta'|^* \lambda'_{11} + \eta_1(\rho^*_{11} - \rho^*_{21}) = |\lambda'|[|\theta|\lambda'_{11} + (\epsilon_{21} - \epsilon_{11})\Delta_1]$

Substituting from (53) into (50) gives

(53a)
$$\hat{X}_1 = \frac{1}{|\theta'|^*} \{[|\theta|\lambda'_{22} + (\epsilon_{12} - \epsilon_{22})\Delta_2]\hat{V}_1$$
$$- [|\theta|\lambda'_{12} - (\epsilon_{12} - \epsilon_{22})\Delta_1]\hat{V}_2\}$$

(53b)
$$\hat{X}_2 = -\frac{1}{|\theta'|^*} \{[|\theta|\lambda'_{21} - (\epsilon_{21} - \epsilon_{11})\Delta_2]\hat{V}_1$$
$$- [|\theta|\lambda'_{11} + (\epsilon_{21} - \epsilon_{11})\Delta_1]\hat{V}_2\}$$

Bearing in mind the assumptions of the proposition, the conclusion follows by inspection of (53).

(b) The conclusion follows by inspection of (53). ∎

PROPOSITION 8: If X_j is sufficiently small and if the jth industry is subject to nonconstant returns to scale, then an increase in either factor endowment raises the output of the other commodity. The outcome is independent of the returns to scale in the other industry and of the nature of interindustrial externalities. The direction of change of the output of the jth industry is generally indeterminate.

Proof. It suffices to consider the case in which λ_{11} goes to zero. In view of (43a), if $\epsilon^1_{11} \neq 0$, then, as λ_{11} goes to zero, $|\theta'|^*$ goes to $-\epsilon^1_{11}(1 - \epsilon^1_{22})\sigma_2 \neq 0$. It then follows from (53b) that $\hat{X}_2/\hat{V}_1$ goes to $\theta_{12}/(1 - \epsilon^1_{22}) > 0$ and that $\hat{X}_2/\hat{V}_2$ goes to $\theta_{22}/(1 - \epsilon^1_{22}) > 0$. On the other hand, $\hat{X}_1/\hat{V}_1$ goes to $[(1 - \epsilon^1_{22})|\theta| + (\epsilon^1_{12} - \epsilon^1_{22})\theta_{12}\sigma_2]/|\theta'|^*$ and $\hat{X}_1/\hat{V}_2$ goes to $[(1 - \epsilon^1_{22})|\theta| - (\epsilon^1_{12} - \epsilon^1_{22})\theta_{22}\sigma_2]/|\theta'|^*$, both limits being of indeterminate sign. ∎

REFERENCES

Herberg, H. (1969). On the shape of the transformation curve in the case of homogeneous production functions. *Zeitschrift für die gesamte Staatswissenschaft* **125**, 202–210.

Herberg, H., and Kemp, M. C. (1969). Some implications of variable returns to scale. *Canadian Journal of Economics* **2**, 403–415 (reprinted as Chapter 7 in this volume).

Herberg, H., and Kemp, M. C. (1975). Homothetic production functions and the shape of the production possibility locus: Comment. *Journal of Economic Theory* **11**, 287–288.

Jones, R. W. (1968). Variable returns to scale in general equilibrium theory. *International Economic Review* **10**, 261–272.

Kemp, M. C. (1969). "The Pure Theory of International Trade and Investment." Prentice-Hall, Englewood Cliffs, New Jersey.

Kemp, M. C., and Negishi, T. (1970). Variable returns to scale, commodity taxes, factor market distortions and their implications for trade gains. *Swedish Journal of Economics* **72**, 1–11.

Mayer, W. (1974a). Variable returns to scale in general equilibrium theory: A comment. *International Economic Review* **15**, 225–235.

Mayer, W. (1974b). Homothetic production functions and the shape of the production possibility locus. *Journal of Economic Theory* **8**, 101–110.

Meade, J. E. (1952). External economics and diseconomies in a competitive situation. *Economic Journal* **62**, 54–67.

Melvin, J. R. (1969). Increasing returns to scale as a determinant of trade. *Canadian Journal of Economics* **3**, 389–402.

Negishi, T. (1972). "General Equilibrium Theory and International Trade." North-Holland Publ., Amsterdam.

Panagariya, A. (1980). Variable returns to scale in general equilibrium theory once again. *Journal of International Economics* **10**, 499–526.

Tawada, M. (1980). Properties of the set of production possibilities. Doctoral thesis, University of New South Wales.

Horst Herberg[7]
INSTITUT FÜR INDUSTRIE- UND GEWERBEPOLITIK
UNIVERSITÄT HAMBURG
HAMBURG, WEST GERMANY

Murray C. Kemp
SCHOOL OF ECONOMICS
UNIVERSITY OF NEW SOUTH WALES
KENSINGTON, NEW SOUTH WALES
AUSTRALIA

Makota Tawada
DEPARTMENT OF ECONOMICS
KOBE UNIVERSITY OF COMMERCE
TARUMI, KOBE
JAPAN

[7] Present affiliation: Institut für Theoretische Volkswirtschaftslehre, Christian-Albrechts-Universität zu Kiel, Kiel, West Germany.

9

The production-possibility set with public intermediate goods*

MAKOTO TAWADA

1. INTRODUCTION

It is well known that the set of feasible net production points is convex if the underlying production functions are of the constant-returns, no-joint-products type and if there are no technological externalities (see, for example, Herberg and Kemp, 1969). However the upper boundary of the set (that is, the transformation surface) is not necessarily strictly concave; it may contain linear segments or, more generally, flats of dimension possibly greater than one. Recently it has been shown that the degree of flatness is related to the rank of the matrix of primary factor inputs. Specifically, it has been shown that if at any point P in the transformation surface there are s industries active, then the surface contains an $(s-r)$-dimensional flat embracing P if and only if at P there are exactly r linearly independent vectors of primary-factor inputs. As a corollary, if the number of primary factors is less than s, then P necessarily lies in a flat of dimension at least one (see Kemp *et al.*, 1978).

* I am deeply grateful to Professor M. C. Kemp for his kind instruction and suggestions. This chapter first appeared in *Econometrica*, May 1980.

ISBN 0-12-404140-X

We now complicate the world of Kemp, Khang, and Uekawa by adding public intermediate goods. It is shown that if all production functions are of the constant-returns, strictly quasi-concave kind, and if at least one public intermediate good is essential to the output of each final good, then the set of production possibilities is convex and the transformation surface strictly concave, and that this is so whatever the numbers of primary factors, final goods, and public intermediate goods. This conclusion is a striking one, the more so since the publicness of the intermediate goods might have been thought to impart to production an element of increasing returns.

2. ASSUMPTIONS

Let n final goods be produced by means of m primary factors and q public intermediate goods, where n, m, and q are positive but otherwise arbitrary. The nonnegative n-vector of final-good outputs is denoted by $y \equiv (y_1, \ldots, y_n)$ and the nonnegative q-vector of public-good outputs is denoted by $r \equiv (r_1, \ldots, r_q)$. The amount of the kth primary factor employed in producing the ith final good is denoted by v_{ki} and the amount employed in the jth public-good industry by v_{kj}^r. The ith final-good production function, defined on E_+^{m+q}, the nonnegative orthant of $(m + q)$-dimensional Euclidean space, may be written as

$$(1) \qquad\qquad y_i = f^i(z^i) \equiv f^i(v^i, r), \qquad i = 1, \ldots, n$$

where $v^i \equiv (v_{1i}, \ldots, v_{mi})$; and the ith public-good production function, defined on E_+^m, may be written as

$$(2) \qquad\qquad r_j = g^j(v^{rj}), \qquad j = 1, \ldots, q$$

where $v^{rj} \equiv (v_{1j}^r, \ldots, v_{mj}^r)$.

For the time being it is assumed that

(A)   (i) f^i and g^j are positively homogeneous of degree one in all their arguments and possess positive continuous first-order partial derivatives;

(ii)   all inputs are essential, that is, $f^i = 0$ if $z^i \not> 0$ and $g^j = 0$ if $v^{rj} \not> 0$;

(iii) f^i and g^j are strictly quasi-concave in all their arguments.

The assumption that f^i is homogeneous of degree one in z^i (rather than, let us say, in v^i alone[1]) merits an explanation. There are public intermediate goods, of which defense and information are well-known examples, that remain available in full strength to each firm in an economy whatever the number of firms in that economy and whatever their distribution over industries. When public goods are of this type it is reasonable to suppose that the production function for each final good is homogeneous in primary-factor inputs alone. However, there are other intermediate goods that remain available in full strength to a firm whatever the number of firms in other industries but that undergo a reduction in availability to that firm if the number of firms in its own industry expands. Such intermediate goods are incompletely public; they are public between industries but not within industries. Here one thinks of transport and communication networks that can become overloaded in particular regions (or at particular times) and of final-good industries that are regionally (or seasonally) specialized. When intermediate goods are of this semipublic kind, assumption (A)(i) is appropriate.

Let $v \equiv (v_1, \ldots, v_m)$ be the constant vector of primary-factor endowments. Any feasible allocation of primary factors must satisfy

$$(3) \qquad \sum_{i=1}^{n} v^i + \sum_{j=1}^{q} v^{rj} \leqq v$$

The set of feasible outputs is then

$$Y \equiv \{ y \in E_+^n : y_i \leqq f^i(v^i, r) \text{ and } r_j \leqq g^j(v^{rj})$$
$$\text{for some } v^i \geqq 0, \ i = 1, \ldots, n, \text{ and some } v^{rj} \geqq 0,$$
$$j = 1, \ldots, q, \text{ such that } \sum_i v^i + \sum_j v^{rj} \leqq v \}$$

The transformation surface is the upper boundary of Y.

---

[1] This possibility, with $n = 2$ and $m = g = 1$, has been examined by Manning and McMillan (1979). In general, it can be proved that the frontier is convex to the origin in an economy with an arbitrary number of commodities, an arbitrary number of intermediate goods, and one primary factor. The proof is given in Tawada (1980). If there are two primary inputs, the analysis is rather complicated. In this case, it is known that the surface is concave in the neighborhood of both axes under certain restrictions on the production functions (see Tawada, 1980).

3. ANALYSIS

We shall prove the following:

PROPOSITION: If (A) is satisfied, Y is convex and the transformation locus strictly concave.

The proposition follows easily from four lemmas, which we proceed to
state and prove.

LEMMA 1: For any given positive vector $\bar{r} = (\bar{r}_1, \ldots, \bar{r}_q)$ of
outputs of public intermediate goods, the transformation locus is
negatively sloped.

Proof. As is well known, every point on the locus is an optimal
vector of the following problem:

$$(4) \qquad\qquad \max_{v^1, \ldots, v^n, v^{r1}, \ldots, v^{rq}} \sum_i p_i f^i(v^i, \bar{r})$$

subject to

$$\bar{r}_j = g^j(v^{rj}), \qquad j = 1, \ldots, q$$

$$\sum_i v^i + \sum_j v^{rj} = v$$

where $p \equiv (p_1, \ldots, p_n)$ is a semipositive constant vector. Among the
necessary conditions for a maximum of the above problem we have

$$(5) \quad f_k^1/f_l^1 = f_k^i/f_l^i = g_k^j/g_l^j, \quad i = 1, \ldots, n, \ j = 1, \ldots, q, \ k, l = 1, \ldots, m$$

where $f_k^i \equiv \partial f^i/\partial v_{ki}$, $g_k^j \equiv \partial g^j/\partial v_{kj}^r$, etc. On the other hand, differentiating the objective function and the constraints of the above
problem, we obtain

$$(6) \qquad\qquad dy_i = \sum_{k=1}^m f_k^i \, dv_{ki}, \qquad i = 1, \ldots, n$$

$$(7) \qquad\qquad 0 = \sum_{k=1}^m g_k^j \, dv_{kj}^r, \qquad j = 1, \ldots, q$$

and

$$(8) \qquad\qquad 0 = \sum_{i=1}^n dv_{ki} + \sum_{j=1}^q dv_{kj}^r, \qquad k = 1, \ldots, m$$

respectively. From (5) and (6),

(9) $\quad \sum_k f_k^1 \, dv_{ki} = (f_1^1/f_1^i) \sum_k f_k^i \, dv_{ki} = (f_1^1/f_1^i) \, dy_i, \qquad i = 1, \ldots, n$

Summing over i, and applying (7) and (8),

(10) $\quad \sum_i \sum_k f_k^1 \, dv_{ki} = \sum_k f_k^1 \sum_i dv_{ki} = \sum_k f_k^1 (- \sum_j dv_{kj}^r)$

$$= - \sum_j (\sum_k f_k^1 \, dv_{kj}^r) = - \sum_j \left(\frac{f_1^1}{g_1^j} \sum_k g_k^j \, dv_{kj}^r \right) = 0$$

From (9) and (10),

$$\sum_i (f_1^1/f_1^i) \, dy_i = 0$$

so that

(11) $\qquad \partial y_1/\partial y_i \big|_{r=\bar{r}} = -f_1^1/f_1^i, \qquad i = 1, \ldots, n$

Finally, from the positive marginal productivities,

(12) $\qquad\qquad -f_1^1/f_1^i < 0$ ∎

Let

$$f^i(z^i) \equiv f^i(v^i, g^1(v^{r1}), \ldots, g^q(v^{rq}))$$

$$\equiv h^i(v^i, v^{r1}, \ldots, v^{rq}) \equiv h^i(V^i), \qquad i = 1, \ldots, n$$

be the reduced-form production function for the ith industry.

LEMMA 2: Y is convex if h^i is quasi-concave as well as positively linear homogenous in V^i, $i = 1, \ldots, n$.

Proof. Let $y^s \equiv (y_1^s, \ldots, y_n^s) \in Y$, $s = 1, 2$, where $y_i^s = h^i(V^{is})$, $i = 1, \ldots, n$; and let $y^\alpha \equiv (1 - \alpha)y^1 + \alpha y^2$ and $V^{i\alpha} \equiv (1 - \alpha)V^{i1} + \alpha V^{i2}$, where $\alpha \in (0, 1)$. Then, from the linear homogeneity of h^i,

$$y_i^\alpha = h^i\big[(y_i^\alpha/y_i^s) V^{is}\big], \qquad i = 1, \ldots, n, \quad s = 1, 2$$

so that the points $(y_i^\alpha/y_i^1)V^{i1}$ and $(y_i^\alpha/y_i^2)V^{i2}$ lie in the same isoproduct surface. Suppose that h^i is quasi-concave. Then[2] for all $\gamma \in (0, 1)$,

$$y_i^\alpha \leq h^i\big[(1 - \gamma)(y_i^\alpha/y_i^1)V^{i1} + \gamma(y_i^\alpha/y_i^2)V^{i2}\big]$$

---

[2] The quasi-concavity of the functions, together with their positive linear homogeneity, implies the concavity of the functions (see Quirk and Saposnik, 1966; Khang and Uekawa, 1973).

Setting $\gamma = \alpha y_i^1/y_i^\alpha$, we obtain

$$y_i^\alpha \leq h^i(V^{i\alpha}), \qquad i = 1, \ldots, n$$

It is easily verified that $V^{i\alpha}, i = 1, \ldots, n$, satisfy the resource constraints; thus $y_i^\alpha \in Y$ and Y is a convex set. ■

LEMMA 3: If $h^i(V^i)$ is strictly quasi-concave as well as positively linear homogeneous, then the transformation locus is strictly concave.

Proof. Suppose that the transformation surface contains a line segment (y^1, y^2) along which the first n^0 final goods are produced; that is,

$$y_i^s = h^i(V^{is}) > 0, \qquad s = 1, 2, \quad i = 1, \ldots, n^0$$

$$y_i^s = 0, \qquad\qquad s = 1, 2, \quad i = n^0 + 1, \ldots, n$$

Since y^1 and y^2 lie in the transformation surface, and since from (11) and (12) $\partial y_i/\partial y_j$ is negative and finite, there exists a positive n-vector p such that

(13) $$py^1 = py^2$$

Now for any scalar $\alpha \in (0, 1)$ we can define

(14) $$V^{i\alpha} \equiv (1 - \alpha)V^{i1} + \alpha V^{i2}, \qquad i = 1, \ldots, n^0$$

and

(15) $$y_i^\alpha \equiv h^i(V^{i\alpha}), \qquad i = 1, \ldots, n^0$$

Since

$$v_k = \sum_{i=1}^{n^0} v_{ki}^s + \sum_{j=1}^{q} v_{kj}^{rs}, \qquad s = 1, 2, \quad k = 1, \ldots, m$$

we have also

(16) $$v_k = (1 - \alpha)(\sum_{i=1}^{n^0} v_{ki}^1 + \sum_{j=1}^{m} v_{kj}^{r1}) + \alpha(\sum_{i=1}^{n^0} v_{ki}^2 + \sum_{j=1}^{m} v_{kj}^{r2})$$

$$= \sum_{i=1}^{n^0} [(1 - \alpha)v_{ki}^1 + \alpha v_{ki}^2] + \sum_{j=1}^{m} [(1 - \alpha)v_{kj}^{r1}$$

$$+ \alpha v_{kj}^{r2}], \qquad k = 1, \ldots, m$$

implying that $y^\alpha \in Y$. Moreover, h^i is strictly quasi-concave and homogeneous of degree one; hence

(17) $$(1 - \alpha)y^1 + \alpha y^2 \leqq y^\alpha$$

On the other hand, the line segment (y^1, y^2) is in the transformation locus, so that

(18) $$p[(1 - \alpha)y^1 + \alpha y^2] \geqq py^\alpha$$

Finally, from (17) and (18),

(19) $$(1 - \alpha)y^1 + \alpha y^2 = y^\alpha$$

From (19), and the strict quasi-concavity and linear homogeneity of h^i, there exists, for each i, $i = 1, \ldots, n^0$, a positive number $a_i,^3$ not all a_i equal to unity, such that

(20) $$a_i V^{i1} = V^{i2}$$

In fact, from the definition of V^i and the assumption that each public good is essential to the production of each final good, all a_i are the same:

(21) $$a \equiv v^{r1}_{kj}/v^{r2}_{kj} = a_i, \qquad i = 1, \ldots, n^0$$

Without loss of generality, a is taken to be greater than one so that, from (20) and (21),

(22) $$V^{i1} < V^{i2}, \qquad i = 1, \ldots, n^0$$

It follows that

$$v_k = \sum_{i=1}^{n^0} v^1_{ki} + \sum_{j=1}^{q} v^{r1}_{kj} < \sum_{i=1}^{n^0} v^2_{ki} + \sum_{j=1}^{q} v^{r2}_{kj} = v_k$$

which is a contradiction. Hence, if h^i is strictly quasi-concave, the transformation surface cannot contain a line segment and, in view of Lemma 2, must be strictly concave. ∎

To obtain an intuitive understanding of Lemma 3, consider an economy with two final goods, one public intermediate good and one

---

[3] If the function f on R^n is strictly quasi-concave and positively linear homogeneous and if, for two distinct points x^1 and x^2 in R^n and $\alpha \in (0, 1)$,

$$f[\alpha x^1 + (1 - \alpha)x^2] = \alpha f(x^1) + (1 - \alpha)f(x^2)$$

then there is a positive number a such that $x^1 = ax^2$ (see Khang and Uekawa, 1973).

primary factor (labor). In the absence of the intermediate good the transformation surface would be linear (the familiar Ricardian segment). We know that in the presence of a public intermediate good the production set is convex. Suppose that the upper boundary or transformation surface is linear. As the production point moves along the boundary, the labor:public good ratio of the expanding industry must rise relative to the corresponding ratio of the contracting industry. It then follows from the strict quasi-concavity of the production functions that the two marginal rates of factor substitution cannot be equal both before and after the change. Hence the boundary cannot be linear.

LEMMA 4: (i) f^i is strictly quasi-concave in all its arguments and $\partial f^i/\partial r_j > 0$ for $i = 1, \ldots, n$ and $j = 1, \ldots, q$.
(ii) g^j is positively linear homogeneous and strictly quasi-concave in all its arguments.

If (i) and (ii) hold, then h^i is strictly quasi-concave.

Proof. Let $z^{i1} \equiv (v^{i1}, r^1)$ and $z^{i2} \equiv (v^{i2}, r^2)$ be two input vectors for the ith industry and let

$$v^{i\alpha} \equiv (1 - \alpha)v^{i1} + \alpha v^{i2}$$

$$r^\alpha \equiv (1 - \alpha)r^1 + \alpha r^2$$

where $\alpha \in (0, 1)$. Then, since f^i is strictly quasi-concave,

(23) $$f^i(v^{i\alpha}, r^\alpha) \geqq \min\{f^i(v^{i1}, r^1), f^i(v^{i2}, r^2)\}$$

Similarly,

(24) $$v^{rj\alpha} \equiv (1 - \alpha)v^{rj1} + \alpha v^{rj2}, \qquad j = 1, \ldots, q$$

and, since g^j is strictly quasi-concave and linear homogeneous,

(25) $$g^j(v^{rj\alpha}) \geqq (1 - \alpha)g^j(v^{rj1}) + \alpha g^j(v^{rj2})$$
$$= (1 - \alpha)r_j^1 + \alpha r_j^2, \qquad j = 1, \ldots, q$$

Next, from (23)–(25) and the assumption that $\partial f^i/\partial r_j > 0$,

(26) $$h^i(V^{i\alpha}) \equiv f^i[v^{i\alpha}, g^1(v^{r1\alpha}), \ldots, g^q(v^{rq\alpha})]$$
$$\geqq f^i(v^{i\alpha}, r^\alpha)$$
$$\geqq \min\{f^i(v^{i1}, r^1), f^i(v^{i2}, r^2)\}$$
$$= \min\{h^i(V^{i1}), h^i(V^{i2})\}$$

Finally we have to show that (26) holds with strict inequality if $V^{i1} \neq V^{i2}$. Now suppose that $V^{i1} = (v^{i1}, v^{r11}, \ldots, v^{rq1}) \neq V^{i2} = (v^{i2}, v^{r12}, \ldots, v^{rq2})$. If $v^{i1} \neq v^{i2}$, (23) holds with strict inequality, which implies a strict inequality in (26). If $v^{i1} = v^{i2}$, then there must exist at least one index j^* such that $v^{rj^{*}1} \neq v^{rj^{*}2}$. For this j^*, if (25) holds with strict inequality, then (26) holds with strict inequality. If (25) holds with equality, then there is a positive number $b \neq 1$ such that $v^{rj^{*}1} = bv^{rj^{*}2}$. And $r_{j^*}^1 = g^j(v^{rj^{*}1}) = g^j(bv^{rj^{*}2}) = bg^j(v^{rj^{*}2}) = br_{j^*}^2$. This means that $r_{j^*}^1 \neq r_{j^*}^2$. Hence the strict inequality of (23) holds, implying a strict inequality in (26) again. ∎

Having verified the proposition, we notice that not all of our assumptions A(i)–(iii) are needed. In particular, we can dispense with the requirement that each public good is essential to the production of each final good. It suffices that some *one* public good be necessary to the production of each final good.

We notice also that the neglect of nonpublic or private intermediate goods was convenient but not essential. Our proposition remains valid if some or all of the n final goods are also intermediate goods.

REFERENCES

Herberg, H., and Kemp, M. C. (1969). Some implications of variable returns to scale. *Canadian Journal of Economics* **2**, 403–415 (reprinted as Chapter 7 of this volume).

Kemp, M. C., Khang, C., and Uekawa, Y. (1978). On the flatness of the transformation surface. *Journal of International Economics* **8**, 537–542 (reprinted as Chapter 2 of this volume).

Khang, C., and Uekawa, Y. (1973). The production possibility set in a model allowing interindustry flows: The necessary and sufficient conditions for its strict convexity. *Journal of International Economics* **3**, 283–290.

Manning, R., and McMillan, J. (1979). Public intermediate goods, production possibilities, and international trade. *Canadian Journal of Economics* **12**, 243–257.

Quirk, J. F., and Saposnik, R. (1966). Homogeneous production functions and convexity of the production possibility set. *Metroeconomica* **18**, 192–197.

Tawada, M. (1980). The properties of the set of production possibilities. Ph.D. thesis, University of New South Wales (unpublished).

DEPARTMENT OF ECONOMICS
KOBE UNIVERSITY OF COMMERCE
TARUMI, KOBE
JAPAN

10

The scale effect of public goods on production-possibility sets*

RICHARD MANNING

JOHN McMILLAN

1. INTRODUCTION

This chapter characterizes the shape of the set of production possibilities in the presence of public goods that are inputs to production processes. Examples of such public intermediate goods are the production infrastructure (transport and communications services, irrigation, and flood control), pollution control, and technological knowledge.

The first formal analysis of the properties of public intermediate goods was provided by Meade (1952). Meade defined two types of public intermediate goods, which he called, respectively, "atmosphere externalities" and "unpaid factors of production:"

> The atmosphere is a fixed condition of production which remains unchanged for all producers in the industry in question without anyone else doing anything about it, however large or small—within limits—is the scale of operations of the industry. On the

This paper was written while McMillan was visiting Universität Mannheim. Helpful comments of Horst Herberg and Murray Kemp are acknowledged.

Copyright © 1982 by Academic Press, Inc.
All rights of reproduction in any form reserved
ISBN 0-12-404140-X

other hand, the unpaid factor of production is an aid to production which is fixed in amount, and which is therefore available on a smaller scale to each producer in the industry if the number of producers increases. (Meade, 1952, pp. 61–62)

The atmosphere externality, then, is the production analogue of the pure public (consumption) good defined by Samuelson (1954): The use of the public good by one economic agent does not reduce the amount available for the other agents to use. The unpaid factor is a semipublic good, susceptible to congestion or overloading.

Constant returns to scale has a different meaning in each case. For an atmosphere public good, suppose the amount of each primary factor used in a particular industry is doubled. Then, by the nature of the pure public good, each unit of primary factor has as much public good to work with as before; by replication, industry output will double. Thus the appropriate definition of constant returns to scale is a production function linear homogeneous in the primary factors alone, as Manning and McMillan (1979, p. 246) have argued. On the other hand, with unpaid factors, doubling the amount of each primary factor employed in the industry leaves each unit of primary factor with less public input to work with than before. This change in factor proportions will result in industry output increasing, but to less than twice what it was. Constant returns to scale means a production function linearly homogeneous to all inputs, including the public good. Thus, given that the quantity of either type of public input is beyond the control of any individual producer, with atmosphere externalities "there are still constant returns to scale for each individual industry but not for society as a whole," while for unpaid factors "there are still constant returns to scale for society as a whole, though not for the individual industry" (Meade, 1952, p. 56).[1]

The alternative definitions have very different implications for the set of production possibilities. Tawada (1980a) showed that when there are public intermediate goods of Meade's second type (unpaid factors),

---

[1] The first assumption (that production functions are linearly homogeneous in primary factors only) was used in the models of Bergström (1973), McMillan (1978), Manning and McMillan (1979), Khan (1980a), Aislabie (1980), and Pugel (1980); the second (homogeneity in all inputs) was used by Negishi (1979), Khan (1980b), and Tawada (1980a). The implications of the alternative functional forms were contrasted by Hillman (1978) and McMillan (1979).

the production-possibility set is convex and the production-possibility frontier is strictly concave to the origin. This reinforces the usual neoclassical conclusion about the rate of product transformation. In contrast, it was shown by Manning and McMillan (1979) that public intermediate goods of Meade's first type (atmosphere externalities) can give rise to nonconvexities in the set of production possibilities. More precisely, they showed that in the case of one primary factor, one public intermediate good, and two consumption goods, the production-possibility frontier is convex to the origin and that the frontier is indeed strictly convex to the origin provided that the public intermediate good affects the two consumption-good industries differently. Tawada (1980b, pp. 46–54) has generalized the first result to allow for arbitrary numbers of consumption and public intermediate goods. This chapter examines the reason for such contradictory results by setting up a general model of public intermediate goods of which the atmosphere externalities and unpaid-factor externalities are both special cases. Those elements of the model that tend to generate a convex production-possibility set, as well as those which tend to give rise to nonconvexities, are isolated.

The significance of this inquiry is that, as is well known, in an economy with nonconvexities, existence and Pareto-optimality of competitive equilibrium cannot be assured. The free-rider problem means that in an economy with public goods, Pareto optima may not be attainable. When the public goods are intermediate goods rather than consumption goods, this reason for misallocation of resources loses much of its force because the problem of obtaining the information needed to compute how much public-good supply is optimal (information on production functions rather than utility functions) is of lower order of difficulty. If, however, the public intermediate goods give rise to nonconvexities in the production-possibility set, then there is a second source of misallocation of resources, separate from the free-rider problem. With nonconvexities, even if the public intermediate good is optimally supplied by some mechanism, rational action by individual agents may not lead to an efficient outcome.

2. THE $2 \times 1 \times 1$ CASE

In this section we examine the production-possibility frontier for an economy with only two consumption goods, one primary factor (labor), and one public intermediate good. This simple case highlights the causes of differences in the frontier. The general case is considered, using an alternative approach, in the next section.

The production-possibility set Z is defined to be

$$(1) \qquad Z \equiv \{(Y_1, Y_2): Y_i = F_i(L_i, R), i = 1, 2; L_1, L_2 \geq 0;$$

$$R = aL_r; L_r \geq 0; L_1 + L_2 + L_r \leq L\}$$

Y_i is the output of, F_i is the production function for, and L_i is the labor input to the ith consumption-goods industry. R is the quantity of the public intermediate good, which enters the production functions of both consumption-goods industries. L_r is the input of labor into the industry producing the public intermediate good, and a is the output–input coefficient for that industry. The public intermediate good is produced under constant returns to scale from labor alone. L is the total labor supply, which cannot be exceeded by the use of labor in the three industries.

The formulation of Z in (1) is sufficiently general to encompass as special cases the assumptions of Manning and McMillan (1979) and of Tawada (1980a) when his model is restricted to this number of commodities.

It will be assumed that the production functions F_i are quasi-concave and satisfy these restrictions:

$$(2) \qquad F_i \in \mathbf{C}_2; \quad F_i(0, R) = 0; \quad \partial F_i/\partial L_i > 0; \quad \partial F_i/\partial R \geq 0,$$

$$> \text{at least one } i; \quad \partial^2 F_i/\partial R^2 \leq 0; \quad \partial^2 F_i/\partial L_i^2 \leq 0;$$

$$\partial^2 F_i/\partial L_i \, \partial R \geq 0, \, > \text{at least one } i.$$

That is, the production functions are sufficiently differentiable for the method of analysis of this section, while labor is a necessary input. In addition, labor and the public intermediate good are useful inputs, in the sense that they have positive, and nonnegative, marginal products. These marginal products are assumed to be nonincreasing. Finally, an increase in the public intermediate good does not lower the marginal productivity of labor anywhere.

The production-possibility frontier is the upper boundary of Z. It is immediate from (2) that the labor constraint is tight on the frontier [that is, = holds in (1)]. The condition for an efficient supply of the public intermediate good, which is necessary for the economy to reach the production possibility frontier, is

(3)
$$\sum_{i=1}^{2} \frac{\partial F_i/\partial R}{\partial F_i/\partial L_i} = \frac{1}{a}$$

This is the production analog of the familiar summation rule popularized by Samuelson for public consumption goods. It is derived and discussed in Kaizuka (1965), Sandmo (1972), Hillman (1978), and McMillan (1979).

The production functions may be used to express the labor input required to produce a level of output, given the supply of the public input. Thus,

(4)
$$L_i = G_i(Y_i, R), \qquad i = 1, 2$$

Using (4), and recalling that the labor constraint is tight on the production possibility frontier, gives

(5)
$$G_1(Y_1, R) + G_2(Y_2, R) + R/a = L$$

The production-possibility frontier may be found as an envelope. For fixed public intermediate goods supply, (5) defines a locus of combinations of Y_1 and Y_2. For different values of R, a different such locus is defined (in general). The production-possibility frontier is found as the envelope of these loci for all possible values of R. This envelope is defined implicitly by (5) and the efficiency condition (3), as Manning and McMillan (1979, p. 248) have noted in a more restricted case.

Totally differentiating (4) gives

(6)
$$dL_i = \frac{\partial G_i}{\partial Y_i} dY_i + \frac{\partial G_i}{\partial R} dR$$

But totally differentiating the production function, and rearranging, gives

(7)
$$dL_i = \frac{1}{\partial F_i/\partial L_i} dY_i - \frac{\partial F_i/\partial R}{\partial F_i/\partial L_i} dR$$

Therefore

(8)
$$\frac{\partial G_i}{\partial Y_i} = \frac{1}{\partial F_i/\partial L_i} > 0$$

and

(9)
$$\frac{\partial G_i}{\partial R} = - \frac{\partial F_i/\partial R}{\partial F_i/\partial L_i} \leq 0$$

The use of (9) in (3) allows the efficiency condition to be written as

(10) $$\sum_{i=1}^{2} \partial G_i / \partial R + 1/a = 0$$

PROPOSITION 1: The slope of the production-possibility frontier equals the (negative of the) ratio of the marginal products of labor for the efficient supply of the public intermediate good.

Proof. Total differentiation of (5) gives

(11) $$\frac{\partial G_1}{\partial Y_1} dY_1 + \frac{\partial G_1}{\partial R} dR + \frac{\partial G_2}{\partial Y_2} dY_2 + \frac{\partial G_2}{\partial R} dR + dR/a = 0$$

The use of (10) in (11) gives

(12) $$\frac{dY_2}{dY_1} = -\frac{\partial G_1/\partial Y_1}{\partial G_2/\partial Y_2}$$

Then (8) applied to (12) gives

(13) $$\frac{dY_2}{dY_1} = -\frac{\partial F_2/\partial L_2}{\partial F_1/\partial L_1}$$

from which the statement of the proposition is obvious. ∎

From (12) a general expression for the curvature of the production-possibility frontier can be obtained.

PROPOSITION 2: The curvature of the production possibility frontier is given by

(14) $$\frac{d^2 Y_2}{dY_1^2} = \frac{A + B}{C}$$

where

(15) $$A \equiv -\left(\frac{\partial^2 G_1}{\partial R^2} + \frac{\partial^2 G_2}{\partial R^2}\right)\left[\frac{\partial^2 G_1}{\partial Y_1^2}\left(\frac{\partial G_2}{\partial Y_2}\right)^2 + \frac{\partial^2 G_2}{\partial Y_2^2}\left(\frac{\partial G_1}{\partial Y_1}\right)^2\right] \leq 0$$

(16) $$B \equiv \left(\frac{\partial^2 G_1}{\partial Y_1 \partial R}\frac{\partial G_2}{\partial Y_2} - \frac{\partial^2 G_2}{\partial Y_2 \partial R}\frac{\partial G_1}{\partial Y_1}\right)^2 \geq 0$$

(17) $$C \equiv \left(\frac{\partial^2 G_1}{\partial R^2} + \frac{\partial^2 G_2}{\partial R^2}\right)\left(\frac{\partial G_2}{\partial Y_2}\right)^3 > 0$$

Proof. Differentiating (12) and rearranging gives

$$
(18) \quad \frac{d^2 Y_2}{dY_1^2} = -\left[\left(\frac{\partial^2 G_1}{\partial Y_1^2} \frac{\partial G_2}{\partial Y_2} - \frac{\partial^2 G_2}{\partial Y_2^2} \frac{dY_2}{dY_1} \frac{\partial G_1}{\partial Y_1} \right) \right.
$$
$$
\left. + \left(\frac{\partial^2 G_1}{\partial Y_1 \partial R} \frac{\partial G_2}{\partial Y_2} - \frac{\partial^2 G_2}{\partial Y_2 \partial R} \frac{\partial G_1}{\partial Y_1} \right) \frac{dR}{dY_1} \right] \bigg/ \left(\frac{\partial G_2}{\partial Y_2} \right)^2
$$

Differentiating the efficiency condition (10) yields

$$
(19) \quad \frac{dR}{dY_1} = -\left(\frac{\partial^2 G_1}{\partial R \, \partial Y_1} + \frac{\partial^2 G_2}{\partial R \, \partial Y_2} \frac{dY_2}{dY_1} \right) \bigg/ \left(\frac{\partial^2 G_1}{\partial R^2} + \frac{\partial^2 G_2}{\partial R^2} \right)
$$

Substituting for dR/dY_1 from (19) and for dY_2/dY_1 from (12) into (18) gives (14).

From (6) and (7) it can be shown that

$$
(20) \quad \frac{\partial^2 G_i}{\partial Y_i^2} = -\frac{\partial^2 F_i / \partial L_i^2}{(\partial F_i / \partial L_i)^3} \geq 0
$$

$$
(21) \quad \frac{\partial^2 G_i}{\partial Y_i \, \partial R} = \left(\frac{\partial^2 F_i}{\partial L_i^2} \frac{\partial F_i}{\partial R} - \frac{\partial^2 F_i}{\partial L_i \, \partial R} \frac{\partial F_i}{\partial L_i} \right) \bigg/ \left(\frac{\partial F_i}{\partial L_i} \right)^3 < 0
$$

$$
(22) \quad \frac{\partial^2 G_i}{\partial R^2} = \left[-\frac{\partial^2 F_i}{\partial L_i^2} \left(\frac{\partial F_i}{\partial R} \right)^2 + 2 \frac{\partial^2 F_i}{\partial L_i \, \partial R} \frac{\partial F_i}{\partial R} \frac{\partial F_i}{\partial L_i} \right.
$$
$$
\left. -\frac{\partial^2 F_i}{\partial R^2} \left(\frac{\partial F_i}{\partial L_i} \right)^2 \right] \bigg/ \left(\frac{\partial F_i}{\partial L_i} \right)^3 > 0
$$

where (2) is used to obtain the signs. A is nonpositive, in view of (20) and (22). B is squared, and so is nonnegative. C is strictly positive, in view of (22). ∎

The sign of $d^2 Y_2/dY_1^2$, and therefore the local concavity or convexity of the production-possibility frontier, depends on whether the first or second term in the numerator of (14) dominates. The production-possibility frontier is locally concave, linear, or convex as $-A$ exceeds, equals, or is less than B: When the specific cases of Manning and McMillan (1979) and Tawada (1980a) are considered, this comparison can be made.

With public intermediate goods of the atmosphere type, Manning and McMillan (1979, p. 246) have shown that the production function for industry i must be

$$
(23) \quad Y_i = F_i(L_i, R) = A_i(R) L_i
$$

Define the elasticity of the marginal product of labor in industry i with respect to changes in public input supply as

$$(24) \qquad \zeta_i \equiv \frac{(\partial^2 F_i/\partial L_i \, \partial R)R}{\partial F_i/\partial R} = \frac{A_i'(R)R}{A_i(R)}$$

for $i = 1, 2$.

PROPOSITION 3: If public intermediate goods are of the atmosphere type, then the production-possibility frontier is convex to the origin; Indeed it is strictly convex to the origin when $\zeta_1 \neq \zeta_2$ (i.e., when one industry's output is more sensitive to changes in the supply of the public intermediate good than is the other industry's output).

Proof. Equation (23) implies that $\partial^2 F_i/\partial L_i^2 = 0$, $i = 1, 2$. But then (15) and (20) imply that $A = 0$, which according to Proposition 2 implies that

$$(25) \qquad d^2 Y_2/dY_1^2 = B/C \geq 0$$

Moreover, (16), (21), and (23) imply that

$$(26) \quad B = \frac{1}{(\partial F_1/\partial L_1)^2(\partial F_2/\partial L_2)^2}\left(-\frac{\partial^2 F_1/\partial L_1 \, \partial R}{\partial F_1/\partial L_1} + \frac{\partial^2 F_2/\partial L_2 \, \partial R}{\partial F_2/\partial L_2} \right)^2$$

Clearly, recalling (24), (26) implies that

$$(27) \qquad d^2 Y_2/dY_1^2 > 0 \quad \text{if and only if} \quad \zeta_1 \neq \zeta_2$$

The conclusions on the curvature of the frontier follow from (25) and (27). ∎

Proposition 3 was derived, in a less satisfactory way, byManning and McMillan (1979). It contrasts with the result now obtained by supposing the public intermediate good to be an unpaid factor of production [this is the conclusion reached by Tawada (1980a) when applied to the present $2 \times 1 \times 1$ case].

PROPOSITION 4: If the production functions F_i exhibit constant returns to scale, then the production-possibility frontier is strictly concave to the origin.

Proof. Write

$$(28) \qquad A + B = D + (\partial G_2/\partial Y_2)^2 E_1 + (\partial G_1/\partial Y_1)^2 E_2$$

where

(29) $$D \equiv -\left(\frac{\partial G_2}{\partial Y_2}\right)^2 \frac{\partial^2 G_1}{\partial Y_1^2} \frac{\partial^2 G_2}{\partial R^2} - \left(\frac{\partial G_1}{\partial Y_1}\right)^2 \frac{\partial^2 G_2}{\partial Y_2^2} \frac{\partial^2 G_1}{\partial R^2}$$

$$- 2 \frac{\partial^2 G_1}{\partial Y_1 \partial R} \frac{\partial^2 G_2}{\partial Y_2 \partial R} \frac{\partial G_1}{\partial Y_1} \frac{\partial G_2}{\partial Y_2}$$

(30) $$E_i \equiv -\frac{\partial^2 G_i}{\partial R^2} \frac{\partial^2 G_i}{\partial Y_i^2} + \left(\frac{\partial^2 G_i}{\partial Y_i \partial R}\right)^2, \qquad i = 1, 2$$

From (8), (9), (20), (21), and (22), $D < 0$. From (20), (21), and (22),

(31) $$E_i = \frac{1}{(\partial F_i / \partial L_i)^4} \left[-\frac{\partial^2 F_i}{\partial L_i^2} \frac{\partial^2 F_i}{\partial R^2} + \left(\frac{\partial^2 F_i}{\partial L_i \partial R}\right)^2 \right], \qquad i = 1, 2$$

But since F_i is linearly homogeneous and quasi-concave, it is concave, so that

(32) $$\frac{\partial^2 F_i}{\partial L_i^2} \frac{\partial^2 F_i}{\partial R^2} - \left(\frac{\partial^2 F_i}{\partial L_i \partial R}\right)^2 \geq 0, \qquad i = 1, 2$$

This implies that $E_i \leq 0, i = 1, 2$. Hence $A + B < 0$, and Proposition 2 gives the conclusion. ∎

The conclusion of Proposition 4 holds if the production functions F_i are strictly concave. In that case, in place of (32) it happens that

(33) $$\frac{\partial^2 F_i}{\partial L_i^2} \frac{\partial^2 F_i}{\partial R^2} - \left(\frac{\partial^2 F_i}{\partial L_i \partial R}\right)^2 > 0, \qquad i = 1, 2$$

so that $E_i < 0, i = 1, 2$. Of course, $A + B < 0$, which implies the strict concavity of the production-possibility frontier.

Should either of the production functions F_i, $i = 1, 2$, be quasi-concave but exhibit increasing returns to scale to both inputs, then it may happen that the inequality in (33) is reversed (because the quadratic approximation to the production function is indefinite). If so, the negative term D in (28) may be outweighed by one or more positive terms. Thus, these considerations may be summarized as

PROPOSITION 5: It is *sufficient* for the production-possibility frontier to be strictly concave to the origin that both consumption-goods industries exhibit nonincreasing returns to scale in both inputs. It is *necessary* for the production-possibility frontier to be convex to the origin that there be increasing returns to scale to both inputs in at least one industry.

This proposition gives the same importance to the nature of returns to scale in the economy with public intermediate goods as the concept has long enjoyed in economies with purely private goods. In this respect, public intermediate goods add no new features to the relation between the technology of industries and the production-possibility set. However, the concept of a public intermediate good does suggest a specific increasing-returns form for the production functions such that the production-possibility frontier is convex to the origin.

Finally, it is of some interest that the same results hold if R is a public "bad," such as pollution.[2] Replace parts of (2) so that

$$(34) \qquad \frac{\partial F_i}{\partial R} < 0, \qquad \frac{\partial^2 F_i}{\partial R \, \partial L_i} < 0, \qquad \frac{\partial^2 F_i}{\partial R^2} \leq 0, \qquad i = 1, 2$$

That is, R negatively affects production, and increasing R decreases the marginal productivity of labor and increases the marginal damage per unit of R. Then from (20) and (22), $\partial^2 G_i / \partial Y_i^2 \geq 0$ and $\partial^2 G_i / \partial R^2 > 0$. Thus the signs of A, B, and C are the same. In the case equivalent to the atmosphere public good, $\partial^2 G_i / \partial Y_i^2 = 0$ as before and the production-possibility frontier is convex. On the other hand, if the production functions are concave, then the production-possibility frontier is concave.

3. SET-THEORETIC CONSIDERATIONS IN THE GENERAL CASE

The analysis in the previous section is carried out by the same techniques that are used in basic treatments of production-possibility sets when all inputs are private. More powerful set-theoretic techniques have become useful in the case of private goods. Debreu (1959, pp. 37–39) defines a production set for each producer; this set lists all the technically feasible combinations of inputs, measured by negative numbers, and outputs, measured by positive numbers, for this producer. The aggregate production set, which shows the technically feasible inputs and outputs for the economy, is the sum of all the individual sets.

---

[2] The effects of pollution on the shape of the production-possibility frontier have been examined in a somewhat different model from this one by Siebert (1980).

The production-possibility set is derived as a projection of a section of the aggregate production set. Subject to some important modifications, a similar procedure can be applied to the case of public intermediate goods.

The summation of the individual producers' production sets yields the aggregate production set because of the additive nature of private goods: The total supply of a private good must be parceled out among its users. This contrasts with the case of a public intermediate good, which is available to everyone in whatever total quantity it is made available. The production sets of individual producers ("industries") may be defined in the usual way,[3] but it is not their sum that gives the aggregate production set, since some components are not naturally additive. This is now explored formally.

There are two classes of commodities, private goods and public intermediate goods. The number of these is $m + n$ and r, respectively. Of the private goods m are produced, and n are natural resources in fixed supply. The commodity space is R^{m+n+r}.

The production set of the ith industry producing private goods is $Y_i \subseteq R^{m+n+r}$. Y_i shows all technically feasible combinations of inputs and outputs. Inputs are shown by negative numbers, and outputs by positive numbers. In particular, the last $n + r$ components of any $y_i \in Y_i$ are nonpositive, and at least one of these components is negative. That is, either a resource or a public intermediate good must be used as an input. Let there be s such industries.

Suppose that there is a single industry producing public intermediate goods. Let its production set be $T \subseteq R^{m+n+r}$. Inputs and outputs are represented by negative and positive numbers, respectively. In particular, the last r components of any $t \in T$ are nonnegative, while

---

[3] But as Milleron (1972) noted, to capture formally the idea that public intermediate goods do not disappear when the consumption-goods industries make use of them, it is necessary that, in each consumption-goods industry's production plan, the public intermediate good appear twice; once with a negative sign and once with a positive sign. It is as if the ith consumption-goods industry produces as joint products the good Y_i and the public good R from inputs of labor L_i and public input R. The addition of individual production sets causes the $+R$ and $-R$ to cancel out for each industry, and so for the economy, leaving the output of the public good alone available to the economy. However, this does not ensure that all industries use the same quantity of the public intermediate good, unless the production set for that industry is defined in an artificial way; that is, it produces "joint products" in fixed proportions, each one of which is supplied to exactly one consumption-goods industry. It might also be remarked that the inclusion of positive and negative terms *in the same component* of a vector is impossible!

components $1, \ldots, m + n$ are nonpositive, with at least one of these components being negative. That is, at least one of the private goods must be used as an input to this industry.

$Y_1, \ldots, Y_s$ and T may be used to define the aggregate production set Y, as follows:

$$(35) \quad Y \equiv \{y \in R^{m+n+r} : y_i = y_{1i} + \cdots + y_{si} + t_i \, (i = 1, \ldots, m + n);$$

$$y_i = -y_{ki} = t_i \, (k = 1, \ldots, s, i = m + n + 1, \ldots, m + n + r);$$

$$(y_{k1}, \ldots, y_{k,m+n+r}) \in Y_k \, (k = 1, \ldots, s); (t_1, \ldots, t_{m+n+r}) \in T\}$$

The aggregate production set is formed by calculating all technically feasible excess supplies of the private goods (including the natural resources) and requiring of public intermediate goods that the output of each equal the input of each to each private good industry.

PROPOSITION 6: If $Y_1, \ldots, Y_s$ and T are convex, then Y is convex.

Proof. Consider $y^1, y^2 \in Y$. There are $y_i^1, y_i^2 \in Y_i, i = 1, \ldots, s$, and $t^1, t^2 \in T$ such that, for $j = 1, 2$,

$$(36) \quad y_i^j = y_{1i}^j + \cdots + y_{si}^j + t_i^j, \qquad i = 1, \ldots, m + n$$

$$(37) \quad y_i^j = -y_{ki}^j = t_i^j, \qquad\qquad k = 1, \ldots, s,$$

$$i = m + n + 1, \ldots, m + n + r$$

Now consider $y = \lambda y^1 + (1 - \lambda)y^2, 0 \le \lambda \le 1$. Then

$$(38) \quad y_i = \lambda(y_{1i}^1 + \cdots + t_i^1) + (1 - \lambda)(y_{1i}^2 + \cdots + t_i^2)$$

$$(39) \quad y_i = (\lambda y_{1i}^1 + (1 - \lambda)y_{1i}^2) + \cdots + (\lambda t_i^1 + (1 - \lambda)t_i^2),$$

$$i = 1, \ldots, m + n$$

and

$$(40) \quad y_i = -(\lambda y_{ki}^1 + (1 - \lambda)y_{ki}^2) = \lambda t_i^1 + (1 - \lambda)t_i^2,$$

$$k = 1, \ldots, s, \quad i = m + n + 1, \ldots, m + n + r$$

However, $(\lambda y_i^1 + (1 - \lambda)y_i^2) \in Y_i, i = 1, \ldots, s$ and $(\lambda t^1 + (1 - \lambda)t^2) \in T$, since these sets are convex. Therefore $y \in Y$. ∎

The aggregate production set shows what the economy has the technical ability to produce. Not all plans that are technically possible are within the resource limitations confronting the economy, however. There is a fixed endowment L_i of the ith natural resource; the excess demand for the $(m + i)$th commodity must not exceed the endowment of this resource. That is,

$$(41) \quad -y_i \leq L_i, \quad \text{or} \quad y_i \geq -L_i, \quad i = m + 1, \ldots, m + n$$

(remembering that y_i is an excess supply, so that $-y_i$ is the excess demand for commodity i). Each inequality in (41) defines a closed half-space of R^{m+n+r}. Call the ith of these H_i. H_i is convex. Therefore (41) defines a set $H_{m+1} \cap H_{m+2} \cap \cdots \cap H_{m+n} \subseteq R^{m+n+r}$, which is convex. This set shows all the plans that are consistent with the resource limitations of the economy.

Define the set of feasible productions to be

$$(42) \qquad W \equiv H_{m+1} \cap \cdots \cap H_{m+n} \cap Y \subseteq R^{m+n+r}$$

That is, elements of W satisfy both the resource and technical limitations of the economy.

The production-possibility set Z is the projection of W onto the coordinate subspace of the produced commodities.

PROPOSITION 7:   The production-possibility set Z is convex if $Y_1, \ldots, Y_s$, and T are convex.

Proof. Y is convex, in view of Proposition 6. W defined in (42) is convex, as the intersection of convex sets. Z is a projection of W. But the projection of a set is a linear mapping. Linear mappings preserve convexity, so Z is convex. ∎

This result verifies in a general setting that convexity in individual production sets generates convexity in the production-possibility set, even in the presence of public intermediate goods. Tawada (1980a) obtained a stronger result, that the production-possibility frontier is strictly concave to the origin. His assumptions on the technology are a special case of those given in this section. He assumed that individual industries production functions have constant returns to scale. The analog here is that the individual production sets are convex cones with vertex 0. On the other hand, Manning and McMillan (1979) make an assumption on the production functions that is equivalent to nonconvex industrial production sets. It follows that the aggregate production set Y is nonconvex, and so are W and Z, in general.

4. CONCLUSION

Public intermediate goods confer benefits on all firms and industries. To the extent that further firms or industries can enjoy a public intermediate good, the cost of providing it can be spread more thinly, and it would be expected that this would impart an increasing returns-to-scale effect to production possibilities. This chapter has shown that production-possibility sets are nonconvex only if the public intermediate good causes increasing returns in an individual industry. There are no tendencies toward the nonconvexity of production possibilities due to a commodity being an input to more than one industry. Inputs with the properties that Tawada (1980a) has ascribed to public intermediate goods do not impart any increasing returns effect to production-possibility sets.

Whether the production-possibility frontier is concave or convex to the origin is an empirical matter. It depends on the nature of returns to scale to all inputs at the level of each industry. The importance of settling this question stems from the possibilities that the shape of the production-possibility frontier dictates for the optimal pricing of commodities, including the public intermediate good.

The production-possibility frontier is in part defined by the Samuelson condition; unless the public input is optimally supplied, the economy will not operate on its production-possibility frontier. If the firms in the economy are competitive, then each will be such a small part of the industry that none will find it in its interest to supply the public intermediate good in anything approaching its efficient quantity; there is a role for a beneficent government to supply it. If the production-possibility frontier is concave, then it is enough that the public good be supplied in an efficient quantity; competitive firms will ensure that production takes place at the welfare-maximizing point on the production-possibility frontier. If, however, the production-possibility frontier is convex, then prices will give firms the "wrong" signals. For welfare maximization it is necessary not only that the public good be supplied efficiently but also that there be an appropriate tax-subsidy scheme to counter the effects of the economies of scale.

REFERENCES

Aislabie, C. (1980). The provision of public factors in on "active" industrial policy (mimeographed). Department of Economics, University of Newcastle.

Bergström, T. C. (1973). On efficient provision of social overhead goods. *Yearbook of East-European Economics* **4**, 11–41.

Debreu, G. (1959). "The Theory of Value: An Axiomatic Analysis of Economic Equilibrium." Wiley, New York.

Hillman, A. L. (1978). Symmetries and asymmetries between public-input and public-good equilibria. *Public Finance* **33**, 269–279.

Kaizuka, K. (1965). Public goods and decentralisation of production. *Review of Economics and Statistics* **47**, 118–120.

Khan, M. A. (1980a). A factor price and public input equalization theorem. *Economics Letters* **5**, 1–6.

Khan, M. A. (1980b). "Public Inputs and the Pure Theory of Trade," Working Paper No. 59. Department of Political Economy, Johns Hopkins University, Baltimore, Maryland.

McMillan, J. (1978). A dynamic analysis of public intermediate goods supply in an open economy. *International Economic Review* **19**, 665–677.

McMillan, J. (1979). A note on the economics of public intermediate goods. *Public Finance* **34**, 293–299.

Manning, R., and McMillan, J. (1979). Public intermediate goods, production possibilities, and international trade. *Canadian Journal of Economics* **12**, 243–257.

Meade, J. E. (1952). External economies and diseconomies in a competitive situation. *Economic Journal* **62**, 54–67. [Reprinted in "Readings in Welfare Economics" (K. J. Arrow and T. Scitovsky, eds.), Irwin, Illinois, 1969.]

Milleron, J.-C. (1972). Theory of value with public goods: A survey article. *Journal of Economic Theory* **5**, 419–477.

Negishi, T. (1979). "Microeconomic Foundations of Keynesian Macroeconomics." North-Holland Publ., Amsterdam.

Pugel, T. (1980). "Endogenous Technical Change and International Technology Transfer in a Ricardian Model," Working Paper No. 80–75. Graduate School of Business Administration, New York University, New York.

Samuelson, P. A. (1954). The pure theory of public expenditure. *Review of Economics and Statistics* **36**, 387–389.

Sandmo, A. (1972). Optimality rules for the provision of collective factors of production. *Journal of Public Economics* **1**, 149–157.

Siebert, H. (1980). "Negative Externalities, Environmental Quality and the Transformation Surface," Discussion Paper 157-80. Institut für Volkswirtschaftslehre und Statistik, Universität Mannheim.

Tawada, M. (1980a). The production possibility set with public intermediate goods. *Econometrica* **47**, 1005–1012 (reprinted as Chapter 9 of this volume).

Tawada, M. (1980b). Properties of the set of production possibilities. Ph.D. thesis, University of New South Wales (unpublished).

Richard Manning
DEPARTMENT OF ECONOMICS
UNIVERSITY OF CANTERBURY
CHRISTCHURCH, NEW ZEALAND

John McMillan
DEPARTMENT OF ECONOMICS
UNIVERSITY OF WESTERN ONTARIO
LONDON, ONTARIO
CANADA

11

Exhaustible resources and the set of feasible present–value production points*

MURRAY C. KEMP

MAKOTO TAWADA

1. INTRODUCTION

Pervading the literature on production sets, and common to all other chapters in the present volume, is the assumption that all primary or nonproduced factors of production are inexhaustible. The assumption is both highly restrictive and implausible. Its popularity can be explained partly in historical terms: with a few well-known exceptions, economic theorists have been interested in the implications of exhaustibility for little more than a decade. But perhaps another part of the explanation can be found in the fact that, when resources are exhaustible, there may not exist a vector of positive steady-state production rates, that is, production rates that can be maintained indefinitely. In this chapter we seek to avoid this difficulty by focusing on the set of feasible *present-value* production points or, in the special case in which no discount is applied, on the set of feasible *cumulative* production points.

* We are indebted to Ngo Van Long for several useful comments.

We proceed to define the set of feasible present-value production points, draw out several of its properties, and show by example that it can be a useful tool in resource economics.

2. PROPERTIES OF THE SET OF PRODUCTION POINTS

Consider a closed economy with l inexhaustible primary factors of production, the available endowment of which may vary from period to period; with m exhaustible resources, the extent of which is known at the outset; and with n final products. Suppose further that the economy runs for T periods of time; for the time being, T is taken to be finite. Neglecting produced factors of production, we may write the output y_{it} of the ith commodity in the tth period of time as a function of the l-vector $v_t^i \equiv (v_{1t}^i, \ldots, v_{lt}^i)$ of inputs of inexhaustible primary factors and of the m-vector $r_t^i \equiv (r_{1t}^i, \ldots, r_{mt}^i)$ of inputs of exhaustible primary factors:

(1) $$y_{it} = f_t^i(v_t^i, r_t^i), \qquad i = 1, \ldots, n; \quad t = 0, 1, \ldots, T$$

Notice that the production function for the ith commodity may change from period to period. In a special case, the technology is stationary, so that $f_t^i(\cdot) \equiv f^i(\cdot)$. The production functions are subjected to several restrictions.

(A1)   Each production function possesses a continuous first-order derivative with respect to each of its arguments.

(A2)   Each production function is positively homogeneous of the first degree with respect to all of its arguments.

(A3)   For each i there exists a k such that the kth exhaustible resource is essential to the production of the ith commodity and such that $\partial f^i(v^i, r^i)/\partial r_k^i$, evaluated at $r_k^i = 0$, is finite.

It follows from (A3) that $y_{it} = 0$ if $r_t^i = 0$.

(A4)   Each production function is weakly quasi-concave with respect to all of its arguments.

Introducing the constant discount factor λ $(0 < \lambda \leq 1)$, the present value of the sequence of outputs of the ith commodity is

(2) $$y_i^T \equiv \sum_{t=0}^{T} \lambda^t y_{it}$$

and the vector of present-value outputs is $y^T \equiv (y_1^T, \ldots, y_n^T)$. Next we list the period-by-period and overall factor constraints

(3)

$$\sum_{i=1}^{n} v_{jt}^i \leqq v_{jt}, \qquad j = 1, \ldots, l; \quad t = 0, 1, \ldots, T$$

$$\sum_{t=0}^{T} \sum_{i=1}^{n} r_{kt}^i \leqq r_k, \qquad k = 1, \ldots, m$$

where v_{jt} is the endowment of the jth inexhaustible primary factor in the tth period of time and r_k is the initial holding of the kth exhaustible resource. In a special case, the endowment of inexhaustible primary factors is independent of time, so that $v_t \equiv (v_{1t}, \ldots, v_{lt})$ is a constant vector v. Any factor allocation $(v_t^i, r_t^i, i = 1, \ldots, n; t = 0, 1, \ldots, T)$ that satisfies (3) is said to be feasible. The set of feasible present-value production points is then

(4)
$$Y^T \equiv \{y^T \in R_+^n : (1)\text{--}(3) \text{ are satisfied}\}$$

Evidently $Y^T \subseteq Y^{T+s}$ for all $s \geqq 0$. The present-value production frontier or transformation surface is the upper boundary $\overline{Y}^T$ of Y^T. Any feasible allocation of factors such that y^T is in $\overline{Y}^T$ will be said to be efficient.

The above many-period model of single-country production is formally very similar to Tawada's steady-state many-country model of world production (see Tawada, 1978). To verify that this is so one need only (i) reinterpret the typical country's endowment of immobile primary factors as the typical time period's endowment of inexhaustible primary factors, (ii) reinterpret the typical country's endowment of internationally mobile primary factors as the typical time period's endowment of intertemporally mobile exhaustible resources, and (iii) reinterpret the typical country's production function for the ith commodity as the typical time period's production function for that commodity (with the discount factor λ^t incorporated in the typical time period's production function). Of course, exhaustible resources are intertemporally mobile only in one direction; a resource deposit first available in the tth period of time cannot be made available to an earlier period. To that extent, the correspondence between Tawada's system and ours is incomplete. From our present point of view, however, this is immaterial; for in our formulation all exhaustible resources are available at the outset, so only one-way mobility is needed. On the other hand, the restrictions placed by Tawada on the n production functions are in some respects more severe and in other respects less severe than (A1)–(A4). However, the differences are, once more, inconsequential. For Tawada's lemma, which is what most interests us in his paper, can be proved as easily under (A1)–(A4) as under his own assumptions. Thus, transplanting the lemma, we have

LEMMA 1:   The set of production points Y^T is bounded above, closed, and convex.

We proceed to state two propositions relating to special cases.

LEMMA 2:   Suppose that the endowment of inexhaustible primary factors is independent of time and that the factor allocation $(v_t^i, r_t^i; i = 1, \ldots, n; t = 0, 1, \ldots, T)$ is feasible. Then the constant allocation

$$\left(\bar{v}^i \equiv \sum_{t=0}^{T} v_t^i/(T + 1), \bar{r}^i \equiv \sum_{t=0}^{T} r_t^i/(T + 1); \; i = 1, \ldots, n; \; t = 0, 1, \ldots, T \right)$$

also is feasible.

Proof.   We have

$$\sum_i \bar{v}^i = \sum_i \sum_t v_t^i/(T + 1) = \sum_t \sum_i v_t^i/(T + 1)$$

$$\leq \sum_t v_t/(T + 1) \qquad \text{(by assumption)}$$

$$= v \quad \blacksquare$$

LEMMA 3:   Suppose that the endowment of inexhaustible primary factors is independent of time, the technology is stationary, and the discount factor λ is equal to one (so that the rate of discount is zero). Suppose further that the factor allocation $(v_t^i, r_t^i; \; i = 1, \ldots, n; \; t = 0, 1, \ldots, T)$ is efficient. Then the constant allocation $(\bar{v}^i \equiv \sum_t v_t^i/(T + 1), \bar{r}^i \equiv \sum_t r_t^i/(T + 1); i = 1, \ldots, n; t = 0, 1, \ldots, T)$ also is efficient.

Proof.   From Lemma 2, the constant allocation is feasible; and from (A4),

$$f^i(\bar{v}^i, \bar{r}^i) \geq \sum_t f^i(v_t^i, r_t^i)/(T + 1) \quad \blacksquare$$

To this point it has been assumed that T is finite. We now relax that assumption. This immediately brings into question the boundedness of Y^T as T goes to infinity. Evidently boundedness cannot be secured without some restrictions on the permitted period-by-period changes in technology and in the endowments of inexhaustible primary factors of production.

LEMMA 4: Suppose that the endowment of inexhaustible primary factors is independent of time, the technology is stationary, and $\lambda = 1$. Then as T goes to infinity the production set Y^T approaches a finite limit set Y^∞.

Proof. It suffices to consider the case in which, for all T, $y_i^T = 0$, $i = 2, \ldots, n$. Moreover, in view of Lemma 3 we may confine our attention to the constant allocations

$$v_t^1 = \bar{v}^1 = v, \qquad r_t^1 = \bar{r}^1 = r/(T + 1); \qquad t = 0, 1, \ldots, T$$

$$v_t^i = 0, \qquad r_t^i = 0; \qquad i = 2, \ldots, n; \quad t = 0, 1, \ldots, T$$

Let the kth resource be essential to the production of the first commodity. Then, in view of (A3), we can apply l'Hôpital's rule and deduce that

$$\lim_{r_k/T \to \infty} \frac{f^1(v, r_1, \ldots, r_{k-1}, r_k/T, r_{k+1}, \ldots, r_m)}{r_k/T}$$

is finite. It follows that

$$\lim_{T \to \infty} Tf^i(v, r_1, \ldots, r_{k-1}, r_k/T, r_{k+1}, \ldots, r_m)$$

is finite. On the other hand, clearly

$$f^1(v, r/T) \leq f^1(v, r_1, \ldots, r_{k-1}, r_k/T, r_{k+1}, \ldots, r_m)$$

Hence

$$\lim_{T \to \infty} Tf^1(v, r/T)$$

exists. ■

The conclusion of Lemma 4 remains valid if for all t there is a bound on v_t that is independent of t; to see that this is so, one need only take $(\sup_t v_{1t}, \ldots, \sup_t v_{lt})$ as the endowment of exhaustible primary factors in Lemma 4. And the conclusion of the lemma holds *a fortiori* if $\lambda < 1$. Thus we have the following:

THEOREM: If the technology is stationary and if for the periodic endowments of exhaustible primary factors there is a common bound, then, whether the rate of discount be positive or zero, the limit set Y^∞ exists and is convex.

Remark 1. Y^T invariably contains $\bar{Y}^T$ if T is finite. But Y^∞ does not necessarily contain its upper boundary $\bar{Y}^\infty$. As a counter example we may cite Gale's cake-eating economy with $\lambda = 1$ (see Gale, 1967).

Remark 2. We have worked in discrete time. However, there presumably exists a continuous-time counterpart to the theorem. Suppose that both the endowment of inexhaustible primary factors and the technology are stationary; and recall that along a stationary efficient allocation commodity prices are constant. Then, defining the (rate of flow of) net national product at the initial point of time as

$$P_0 \equiv \sum_{i=1}^{n} p_i y_{i0} - \sum_{k=1}^{m} \mu_{k0} r_{k0}$$

where p_i is the price of the ith commodity and y_{i0} is the (time rate of) output of the ith commodity, r_{k0} is the (time rate of) depletion of the kth exhaustible resource, and μ_{k0} is the shadow price of the kth exhaustible resource, all at the initial point of time, we may apply a theorem of Weitzman (1976) and write

$$P_0 = \rho \sum p_i y_i^\infty (p_1, \ldots, p_n) \equiv \rho \cdot p \cdot y^\infty(p)$$

where ρ is the constant instantaneous rate of interest and $y^\infty(p)$ is the point on $\bar{Y}^\infty$ that will be chosen either by a competitive economy or by a benevolent and perfectly well-informed central planner.

3. APPLICATION

Consider a small country facing given and constant world prices for the n final goods and able to borrow and lend freely at a given and constant world one-period rate of interest. For such a country it will be optimal to maximize the present value of its stream of outputs and then choose a consumption path consistent with the implied budget constraint. The maximum (or, more accurately, the supremum) of the present value of output is found at the point of tangency $\hat{y}^\infty$ of $\bar{Y}^\infty$ and the given and constant price plane.

Kemp and Long (1979) have shown that when $l = 1 = m$ and $n = 2$ the production point $\hat{y}^\infty$ associated with any price ratio is unique. It follows that in that case the production frontier $\bar{Y}^\infty$ is strictly concave.

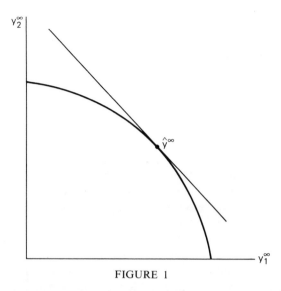

FIGURE 1

Figure 1 provides the familiar illustration. Kemp and Long have shown also that, provided only that each commodity is produced over some nondegenerate interval of time, a small increase in the initial stock of the resource gives rise to a reduction in the cumulative discounted output of the resource-unintensive good and to an increase in the cumulative discounted output of the resource-intensive good, with the

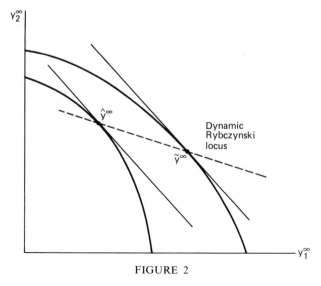

FIGURE 2

proportionate increase in output greater than the proportionate increase in resource stock. In terms of Fig. 2, with the first good taken to be relatively resource intensive, an increase in the resource stock transfers production from point $\hat{y}^\infty$ to point $\bar{y}^\infty$.

4. FINAL REMARKS—RENEWABLE RESOURCES

In Section 2 we considered how the notion of a production set may be redefined to allow for the exhaustibility of some resources. After noting the possible nonexistence of nontrivial steady states, we developed the concept of a set of feasible present-value production sets and obtained sufficient conditions for the convexity and boundedness of the set. Throughout the calculations, however, our attention was confined to *nonreproducible* exhaustible resources, thus leaving as an open question the fate of the notion of a production set when all exhaustible resources are reproducible, either naturally or artificially. In those alternative circumstances, and if the technology and primary-factor endowments are stationary, nontrivial steady states are feasible. In this final section we consider, briefly and in a very sketchy way, the properties of such states when resources naturally renew themselves.

It is supposed that the kth resource grows and declines according to the renewal function

$$\phi_k(r_{1t}, \ldots, r_{mt}), \qquad k = 1, \ldots, m$$

where r_{kt} is now the amount of the kth resource stock at the beginning of period t and ϕ_k is the periodical natural growth of the kth resource stock. Confining our attention to steady states (and therefore dropping the subscript t), we may pose the problem

$$\max_{r_1, \ldots, r_m} Z$$

subject to

$$\phi_k(r_1, \ldots, r_m) \geq \lambda_k Z, \qquad k = 1, \ldots, m$$

$$r_k \geq 0, \qquad k = 1, \ldots, m$$

where all λ_k are nonnegative, with at least one positive, and then, by varying the λ_k, obtain the set of feasible steady-state extraction points that would be feasible if extraction were costless. The set is defined by the inequality

$$(5) \qquad\qquad \psi(e_1, \ldots, e_m) \leq 0$$

where e_k is the rate of extraction of the kth resource.

But extraction *is* costly; it requires the application of scarce primary factors. Hence the locus $\psi = 0$ merely places an upper bound on the set of feasible steady-state extraction points. To make further progress we write

$$(6) \qquad\qquad e_k \leq f^k(v^k), \qquad k = 1,\ldots,m$$

where the production function f^k is subject to the same restrictions as in Section 2, and recall the period-by-period overall factor constraints

$$(7) \qquad\qquad \sum_{k=1}^{m} v_j^k \leq v_j, \qquad j = 1,\ldots,l$$

Between them, (6) and (7) define the set of steady-state extraction points that would be feasible if each resource stock were infinite, that is, if the restriction (5) could be ignored. The true set of feasible steady-state extraction points may then be defined as

$$Y \equiv \{e \equiv (e_1,\ldots,e_m) : (5)\text{--}(7) \text{ are satisfied}\}$$

and the production transformation locus as the upper boundary $\bar{Y}$ of Y. At any point on $\bar{Y}$ the constraints (5) or the constraints (7), or both, may hold with strict equality. Figure 3 illustrates the simple case in which there are just two deposits. The transformation locus is ABC. If extraction lies on the segment AB, but not at B, then at least one primary factor is less than fully utilized. If extraction lies on the segment BC, but not at B, then at least one resource stock is larger than it

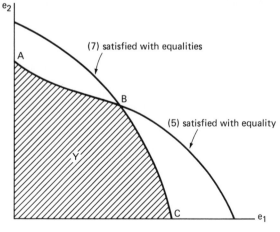

FIGURE 3

need be. The segment AB need not be uniformly concave although, presumably, concavity can be assured by imposing suitable restrictions on the renewal functions ϕ_k. The segment BC may be straight over part or all of its length.

The foregoing very simple account of the set of extraction points rests on the separability of the constraints (5) and (6)–(7). The analysis becomes more complicated if, for example, the cost of extraction depends on the levels of the several resource stocks. For then the constraints (6) must be rewritten as

$$e_i \leqq f^i(r, v^i)$$

and the two sets of constraints intertwine. Similarly, complications appear if the extracted resource is not a final consumption good but a raw material. If costs of extraction are zero, the constraints are then, in obvious notation,

$$y_i \leqq f^i(r^i, v^i), \qquad i = 1, \ldots, n$$

$$\sum_{i=1}^{n} v^i \leqq v, \qquad \sum_{i=1}^{n} r^i \leqq e, \qquad \psi(e) \leqq 0$$

Evidently much work remains.

REFERENCES

Gale, D. (1967). Optimal development in a multi-sector economy. *Review of Economic Studies* **34**, 1–18.

Kemp, M. C., and Long, N. V. (1979). International trade with an exhaustible resource: A theorem of Rybczynski type. *International Economic Review* **20**, 671–677 (reprinted as Essay 13 in "Exhaustible Resources, Optimality, and Trade," M. C. Kemp and N. V. Long, eds., North-Holland Publ., Amsterdam).

Tawada, M. (1978). "On the Shape of the World Production Frontier." School of Economics, University of New South Wales (reprinted as Chapter 4 of the present volume).

Weitzman, M. L. (1976). On the welfare significance of national product in a dynamic economy. *Quarterly Journal of Economics* **90**, 156–162.

Murray C. Kemp
SCHOOL OF ECONOMICS
UNIVERSITY OF NEW SOUTH WALES
KENSINGTON, NEW SOUTH WALES
AUSTRALIA

Makoto Tawada
DEPARTMENT OF ECONOMICS
KOBE UNIVERSITY OF COMMERCE
TARUMI, KOBE
JAPAN

12

Some properties of the per capita production set in the two–sector model of economic growth

*NGO VAN LONG**

1. INTRODUCTION

The two-sector model of economic growth is of special interest because it is simple enough to be manageable yet rich enough to yield a variety of results. However, the usual way in which economic theorists handle this model is far from being the most efficient: the static efficiency conditions (the full employment of both factors and the equality of the marginal rates of substitution) are derived over and over again,[1] when the authors' main task is to study issues such as the uniqueness of momentary equilibrium prices and outputs or the existence, uniqueness, and stability of long-run equilibria in descriptive growth models, or optimal growth models. In this chapter we derive the properties of the per capita production set (relating two outputs per head to capital per head) and show that the resulting per capita production function considerably simplifies the study of the two-sector growth model. We shall also show that the model can be adapted to study problems of economic growth (or decay) with natural resources.

* I wish to thank Murray C. Kemp for many helpful comments.

[1] See, for example, Drandakis (1963), Uzawa (1961), Srinivasan (1964), and Hague (1970).

145

2. PROPERTIES OF THE PER CAPITA PRODUCTION SET

We assume that there are two factors, denoted K and L, and two goods, denoted X_1 and X_2. The production functions of the two goods are denoted $F_1(K_1, L_1)$ and $F_2(K_2, L_2)$. We shall make a number of assumptions concerning these production functions.

ASSUMPTION A.1: $F_i(K_i, L_i)$ is defined for all $K_i \geq 0$, $L_i \geq 0$. $F_i(0, 0) = 0$. $F_i(K_i, L_i) > 0$ for some $(K_i, L_i) > (0, 0)$. $F_i(K_i, L_i)$ is homogeneous of degree one.

The economy's *production set* is

$$P = \{(X_1, X_2, K, L) \in R^4 \mid \exists K_1, L_1, K_2, L_2, \text{and } K_1 + K_2 \leq K,$$

$$L_2 + L_2 \leq L, X_i \leq F_i(K_i, L_i)\}$$

The economy's *per capita production set* is defined as

$$S = \{(x_1, x_2, k) \in R^3 \mid \forall L > 0, (x_1 L, x_2 L, kL, L) \in P\}$$

Clearly, P is a convex cone in R^4, with vertex 0. The set S is therefore a convex set in R^3. As P is closed, so is S.

For any (x_1, k) such that there exists some $x_2 \geq 0$ and $(x_1, x_2, k) \in S$, we define

$$x_2^* = \max\{x_2 \mid (x_1, x_2, k) \in S\}$$

Since x_2^* is unique, we have generated the function

$$x_2^* = g(x_1, k)$$

The function is defined over the domain D, where

$$D = \{(x_1, k) \mid \exists x_2 \geq 0, (x_1, x_2, k) \in S\}$$

The function $g(x_1, k)$ is concave because S is a convex set. To obtain further results, we shall make some additional assumptions.

ASSUMPTION A.2: $F_i(K_i, L_i)$ is strictly quasi-concave and has continuous second-order partial derivatives. In particular,

$$\partial^2 F_i/(\partial K_i)^2 < 0, \qquad \partial^2 F_i/(\partial L_i)^2 < 0$$

ASSUMPTION A.3: $X_i > 0$ implies $(K_i, L_i) > (0, 0)$.

Given Assumptions A.1–A.3, one can define the ratios

$$\rho = L_1/L, \qquad k_i = K_i/L_i$$

and the functions

$$f_i(k_i) = F_i(K_i/L_i, 1)$$

and show that for any $(x_1, k) \in D$, efficiency implies that there exist unique and nonnegative k_1, k_2, ρ, and x_2 satisfying the following equations:

(1) $$x_1 - \rho f_1(k_1) = 0$$

(2) $$x_2 - (1 - \rho)f_2(k_2) = 0$$

(3) $$\rho k_1 + (1 - \rho)k_2 = k$$

(4) $$[f_1(k_1) - k_1 f'_1(k_1)]/f'_1(k_1) = [f_2(k_2) - k_2 f'_2(k_2)]/f'_2(k_2)$$

Our purpose is to relate the derivatives of the functions $g(x_1, k)$ to the variables ρ, k_1, and k_2. The following definitions will be useful:

(5) $$\bar{\omega}_1(k) \equiv [f_1(k) - k f_1(k)]/f'_1(k)$$

(6) $$\bar{\omega}_2(k) \equiv [f_2(k) - k f_2(k)]/f'_2(k)$$

$\bar{\omega}_i(k)$ is the marginal rate of substitution if the country specializes in sector i. Note that Assumption A.2 implies that $\bar{\omega}_i(k)$ is monotonic increasing.

If, at a particular value of k, say k', $\bar{\omega}_i(k') > \bar{\omega}_j(k')$, then we say that sector i is labor-intensive at the endowment ratio k'. If there exists a value of k, say k^*, such that

$$\bar{\omega}_1(k^*) = \bar{\omega}_2(k^*)$$

then k^* is called an *equal intensity endowment ratio*.

Armed with these definitions, we can now state Proposition 1:

PROPOSITION 1: (a)   The function $g(x_1, k)$ is concave, but *not* strictly concave, even if one sector is labor-intensive at all possible endowment ratios.

(b)   The partial derivatives of $g(x_1, k)$ satisfy

(i) $g_k = f'_2(k_2) > 0$,

(ii) $g_{x_1} = -f'_2(k_2)/f'_1(k_1) < 0$,

(iii) $g_{kk} = -A f''_2 f_1^2 f''_1/(f'_1)^2 < 0$,

(iv) $g_{x_1 x_1} = -A(k_1 - k_2)^2 f''_2 f''_1/(f'_1)^2 < 0$,

(v) $g_{x_1 k} = A(k_1 - k_2)f''_2 f_1 f''_1/(f'_1)^2$, $\gtrless 0$ iff $k_1 \gtrless k_2$,

(vi) $g_{x_1 x_1} g_{kk} - (g_{kx_1})^2 = 0$,

where

(7) $(1/A) \equiv -[(\rho f'_1/f'_2)f_2^2 f''_2/(f'_2)^2] - [(1 + \rho)f_1^2 f''_1/(f'_1)^2] > 0$

and

$$f_i \equiv f_i(k_i), \qquad f'_i \equiv f'_i(k_i), \qquad \ldots$$

Proof.   Consider the problem of maximizing

$$x_2 \equiv (1 - \rho)f_2(k_2)$$

subject to

(8) $\rho k_1 + (1 - \rho)k_2 = k$

(9) $\rho f_1(k_1) = x_1$

The choice variables are k_1, k_2, and ρ. The necessary conditions are (8), (9), and

(10) $(f_2/f'_2) - k_2 = (f_1/f'_1) - k_1$

[Of course, (10) and (4) are equivalent expressions.] Differentiating (8)–(10) totally, we obtain

(11) $J \, dz = B \, dv$

where

$$J \equiv \begin{bmatrix} k_1 - k_2 & \rho & 1 - \rho \\ f_1 & \rho f'_1 & 0 \\ 0 & f_1 f''_1/(f'_1)^2 & -f_2 f''_2/(f'_2)^2 \end{bmatrix}$$

$$dz \equiv \begin{bmatrix} d\rho \\ dk_1 \\ dk_2 \end{bmatrix}, \qquad dv \equiv \begin{bmatrix} dx_1 \\ dk \end{bmatrix}, \qquad B \equiv \begin{bmatrix} 0 & 1 \\ 1 & 0 \\ 0 & 0 \end{bmatrix}$$

From (10), $f_1 - k_1 f'_1 - k_2 f'_1 = f_2 f'_1/f'_2$. Using this fact, we can verify that $|J| = -(1/A)$, as defined by (7).

From (11), we obtain

(12) $\partial\rho/\partial x_1 = -A[\rho f_1 f_2 f''_2/(f'_2)^2 + (1 - \rho)f_1^2 f''_1/(f'_1)^2]$

(13) $\partial\rho/\partial k = A\rho f'_1 f_2 f''_2/(f'_2)^2$

(14) $\partial k_1/\partial x_1 = A(k_1 - k_2)f_2 f''_2/(f'_2)^2$

(15) $\partial k_1/\partial k = -Af_1f_2f''_2/(f'_2)^2$

(16) $\partial k_2/\partial x_1 = A(k_1 - k_2)f_1f''_1/(f'_2)^2$

(17) $\partial k_2/\partial k = -Af_1^2f''_1/(f'_1)^2$

In addition, since $x_2 = (1 - \rho)f_2(k_2)$,

(18) $\partial g/\partial k = \partial x_2/\partial k = (1 - \rho)f'_2(\partial k_2/\partial k) - f_2(\partial\rho/\partial k) = f'_2$

(19) $\partial g/\partial x_1 = \partial x_2/\partial x_1 = (1 - \rho)f'_2(\partial k_2/\partial x_1) - f_2(\partial\rho/\partial x_1) = -f'_2/f'_1$

Using (18) and (19) gives

(20) $g_{kk} = f''_2(\partial k_2/\partial k)$

(21) $g_{x_1x_1} = (-f''_2/f'_1)(\partial k_2/\partial x_1) + [f_2f''_1/(f'_1)^2](\partial k_1/\partial x_1)$

(22) $g_{kx_1} = g_{x_1k} = f''_2(\partial k_2/\partial x_1)$

Substituting (17), (16), and (14) into (20)–(22), we obtain the desired results; (iii)–(vi). ∎

Let $G \subseteq R^3$ be the graph of the function $g(x_1, k)$. Proposition 1 suggests that given any point (x_2, x_1, k) on G there exists another point (x'_2, x'_1, k') on G such that the straight line segment joining the two points lies on G, i.e., that the graph of $g(x_1, k)$ is a *ruled surface*. This is made precise by the following proposition:

PROPOSITION 2:   The graph of the function $g(x_1, k)$ is a *ruled surface*. The direction of the straight line segments on the surface is given by

(23) $dk/dx_1 = (k_1 - k_2)/f_1(k_1)$

(24) $dx_2/dx_1 = -f_2(k_2)/f_1(k_1)$

Proof.   From the equation

we obtain the second-order differential of g:

(25) $d^2x_2 = g_{x_1x_1}(dx_1)^2 + g_{kk}(dk)^2 + 2g_{x_1k}(dx_1)(dk)$

Consider two cases:

  (i) $g_{x_1x_1} = 0$ *(implying $g_{x_1k} = 0$)*,
  (ii) $g_{x_1x_1} \neq 0$.

Case (i) obtains iff k is an equal intensity endowment ratio. In this case $d^2x_2 = 0$ iff $dk = 0$; see (25). Now, $dk = 0$ gives

$$dx_2 = g_{x_1}\, dx_1 = (-f'_2/f'_1)\, dx_1$$

Hence the direction of the straight line segment on the surface at an equal intensity endowment ratio is given by

$$\begin{bmatrix} dx_1 \\ dk \\ dx_2 \end{bmatrix} = \begin{bmatrix} dx_1 \\ 0 \\ -(f'_2/f'_2)\, dx_1 \end{bmatrix}$$

Now consider case (ii). Rewrite (25) as

(26) $\qquad d^2x_2 = (g_{x_1x_1})[dx_1 + (g_{x_1k}/g_{x_1x_1})\, dk]^2$
$$- [g_{x_1x_1}g_{x_1k} - (g_{kx_1})^2](dk)^2/g_{x_1x_1}$$

The second term on the right-hand-side of (26) is identically zero, by (vi). Hence $d^2x_2 = 0$ iff

(27) $\qquad dk/dx_1 = -g_{x_1x_1}/g_{x_1k} = (k_1 - k_2)/f_1(k_1)$

Using (27) and the total derivative

$$dx_2 = g_{x_1}\, dx_1 + g_k\, dk$$

we obtain

(28) $\quad dx_2/dx_1 = g_{x_1} + g_k(dk/dx_1) = (-f'_2/f_1) + (k_1 - k_2)(f'_2/f_1)$

Using (10), we can simplify (28) to

(29) $\qquad\qquad dx_2/dx_1 = f_2(k_2)/f_1(k_1).$ ∎

Remark. It is possible to give an alternative proof of Proposition 2 without using the second-order total differential of g. Thus consider any (x_1, k) belonging to the domain of $g(x_1, k)$. Given (x_1, k) there exist unique values of k_1, k_2, ρ and x_2 that satisfy (1)–(4). Define

(30) $\qquad\qquad\qquad x'_1 \equiv x_1 + \epsilon$

for some small ϵ such that

$$\rho' \equiv [\epsilon/f_1(k_1)] + \rho$$

is bounded between 0 and 1. Let

(31) $$k' \equiv k + \epsilon(k_1 - k_2)/f_1(k_1)$$

(32) $$\rho' \equiv (\epsilon/f_1) + \rho$$

(33) $$k'_1 \equiv k_1$$

(34) $$k'_2 \equiv k_2$$

(35) $$x'_2 \equiv (1 - \rho')f_2(k_2) = x_2 - (\epsilon f_2/f_1)$$

It is easily checked that, given x'_1 and k', the values ρ, k'_1, k'_2, x'_2, as defined above, satisfy Eqs. (1)–(4). Hence (x'_1, k'_1, x'_2) is efficient. Thus, given (x_1, k, x_2) on G and the associated values ρ_1, k_1, and k_2, the straight line segment on G passing through (x_1, k, x_2) lies on the intersection of the two planes defined by

(36) $$k' - k = (x'_1 - x_1)(k_1 - k_2)/f_1(k_2)$$

(37) $$x'_2 - x_2 = -(x'_1 - x_1)f_2/f_1$$

Figure 1 illustrates the graph of $g(x_1, k)$. By (33) and (34), marginal products are constant along any straight line segment on the surface. These straight line segments will be called the Rybczynski lines.

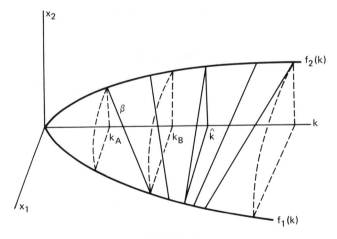

FIGURE 1

3. APPLICATIONS

3.1 *The Descriptive Two-Sector Model of Economic Growth*

Let x_1 be the output of consumption goods and x_2 that of investment goods. (All magnitudes are on a per capita basis.) The *excess demand* for investment goods is given by

$$(38) \quad N(x_1, k) = s_r g_k k + s_w [g(x_1, k) - g_{x_1} x_1 - g\,k] - g(x_1, k)$$

where s_r is the capitalists' propensity to save, $g_k k$ is the capitalists' income (per head), $g(x_1, k) - g_{x_1} x_1$ is the national income (per head) in terms of good 2, $g(x_1, k) - g_{x_1} x_1 - g_k k$ is the wage bill (per head), s_w is the wage earners' propensity to save, and $g(x_1, k)$ is the output of the investment goods.

At any point of time, k is given. If there exists a unique value x_1^* such that the excess demand for good 2 is zero then x_1^* is called the *momentary equilibrium output* of investment goods. Now for given k there exists $\bar{x}_1$ such that $g(\bar{x}_1, k) = 0$. Clearly $N(\bar{x}_1, k) > 0$. Also $N(0, k) < 0$, as $x_1 = 0$ implies a positive excess demand for the consumption goods, hence a negative excess demand for the investment goods. Thus for any given $k > 0$, there exists a value x_1^* at which $N(x_1^*, k) = 0$.

The momentary equilibrium x_1^* is unique if $\partial N / \partial x_1$, evaluated at $x_1^*, k)$, is positive. Now

$$(39) \qquad \partial N / \partial x_1 = k(s_r - s_w)g_{kx_1} - s_w x_1 g_{x_1 x_1} - g_{x_1}$$

It follows that any one of the following conditions is sufficient for the uniqueness of momentary equilibrium:

(i) $k_1 = k_2$,
(ii) $s_r = s_w$,
(iii) $k_1 > k_2$ and $s_r > s_w$,
(iv) $k_1 < k_2$ and $s_r < s_w$.

Another sufficient condition is

(v) $\sigma_1 + \sigma_2 \geq 1$,

where σ_i is the elasticity of substitution in sector i. Any one of the conditions (i)–(iv) is sufficient for the first term in the right-hand-side of (39) to be nonnegative, while condition (v) implies that whenever this term is negative, it is outweighed by the other two terms. While the proof of (v) is rather tedious, the proofs of (i)–(iv), using (39), are straightforward and can be given simple economic interpretations. For example, if (i) holds, we are back to the one-sector model, and hence there exists a unique momentary equilibrium. Consider now the case in which (i) does not hold. In this case any decrease in x_1 for a given k corresponds to an increase in p_2/p_1, which raises the supply of the investment goods. On the other hand, given (ii), a constant proportion of national income is saved; hence as p_2/p_1 increases, national income in terms of the investment goods decreases, causing a fall in the demand for investment goods. Condition (iii) can be linked to the Stolper–Samuelson theorem: if $k_1 > k_2$, an increase in p_2/p_1 will increase the real wage rate and reduce the real rental rate, causing a fall in savings (equal to the demand for the investment goods) provided that $s_r > s_w$. More formally, let S, W, and R stand for real savings, real wage rate, and real rental rate, respectively; then

$$dS = s_r K \, dR + s_w L \, dW = (s_w - s_r)L \, dW$$

(because along the factor price frontier $dR/dW = -L/K$). As a result,

$$dS/dp = (s_w - s_r)L(dW/dp)$$

where $p = p_2/p_1$. Condition (iv) has a similar interpretation.

To summarize, any one of (ii)–(iv) ensures that the demand curve for the investment goods is negatively sloped, while condition (v) ensures that if both curves are positively sloped at an intersection, the demand curve is less steep than the supply curve. Thus the sufficient conditions for the uniqueness of the momentary equilibrium can be explained in terms of demand and supply responses rather than in terms of the technical requirement of "invertibility."

3.2   The Two-Sector Model of Optimal Growth

Let x_2 be the output of the consumption goods, and x_1 be the output of the investment goods. The optimal growth problem posed by Uzawa (1964), Srinivasan (1964), and Hague (1970) consists of finding a path that maximizes

(40)
$$\int_0^\infty e^{-\delta t} g(x_1, k) \, dt$$

subject to

(41) $\dot{k} = x_1 - \mu k$

(42) $x_1 \geq 0$

(43) $x_1 \leq f_1(k)$

The **Hamiltonian** is

(44) $H = g(x_1, k) + \psi(x_1 - \mu k)$

and the Lagrangian is

(45) $L = H + \lambda_1 x_1 + \lambda_2[f_1(k) - x_1]$

The necessary conditions are[2]

(46) $\partial L / \partial x_1 = g_{x_1} + \psi + \lambda_1 - \lambda_2 = 0$

(47) $\lambda_1 \geq 0, \qquad x_1 \geq 0, \qquad \lambda_1 x_1^* = 0$

(48) $\lambda_2 \geq 0, \qquad f_1(k) - x_1 \geq 0, \qquad \lambda_2[f_1(k) - x_1^*] = 0$

(49) $\dot{\psi} = \psi(\delta + \mu) - g_k - \lambda_2 f'_2(k)$

The phase diagram consists of three regions: region N (nonspecialization), region C (specialization in consumption goods), and region I (specialization in investment goods). Figure 2 is a possible diagram. There, it is assumed that $k_1 > k_2$ for $k < \hat{k}$ and $k_1 < k_2$ for $k > \hat{k}$, and that if $f'(k) = \delta + \mu$, then $k < \hat{k}$.

In region N, $\lambda_1 = \lambda_2 = 0$. Hence from (46),

(50) $\partial x_1 / \partial \psi = -1/g_{x_1 x_1} > 0$

(51) $\partial x_1 / \partial k = -g_{x_1 k}/g_{x_1 x_1} \gtrless 0 \qquad$ iff $\quad k_1 \gtrless k_2$

In region C, $\lambda_2 = 0$ and $x_1 = 0$. The curve γ_C separating C from N is given by

$$g_{x_1}(0, k) + \psi = 0$$

and its slope is given by

(52) $d\psi/dk|_{x_1 = 0} = -g_{x_1 k} \gtrless 0 \qquad$ iff $\quad k_2 \gtrless k_1$

From (50), region C is below region N.

---

[2] See, for example, Long and Vousden (1977).

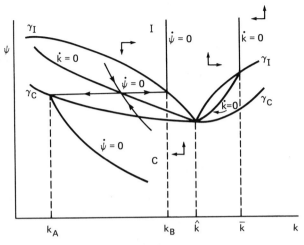

FIGURE 2

In region I, $\lambda_1 = 0$ and $x_1 = f_1(k)$. The curve γ_I separating region I from region N is given by

$$g_{x_1}[f_1(k), k] + \psi = 0$$

and its slope is given by

(53) $d\psi/dk|_{x_1 = f_1(k)} = -g_{x_1 x_1} f_1'(k) - g_{x_1 k} \gtrless 0$ iff $k_2 \gtrless k_1$

In order to have an interior equilibrium, we shall assume that

(54) $$f_1'(0) > \delta + \mu > f_1'(\infty)$$

We are now in a position to determine the shape and position of the curve $\dot\psi = 0$. In region N, $\dot\psi = 0$ iff

(55) $$\psi(\delta + \mu) - g_k(x_1, k) \equiv M(\psi, k) = 0$$

From (55) and (46) we obtain the condition

$$\dot\psi = 0 \Leftrightarrow \delta + \mu = f_1'(k_1)$$

which corresponds to the Rybczynski line β in Fig. 1, where k_B is defined by

(56) $$f_1'(k_B) = \delta + \mu$$

Along the Rybczynski line β both f_1' and f_2' are constant, hence g_k is a constant, implying, by (55), that ψ is a constant. Thus the curve

$\dot{\psi} = 0$ is horizontal in region N; see Fig. 2, where it is assumed that at the endowment ratio $k = k_B$, as defined by (56), the investment goods industry is more capital-intensive. The other case can be handled in a similar fashion.

In region N, $\dot{\psi} < 0$ above the curve $\dot{\psi} = 0$ because

$$\partial \dot{\psi}/\partial \gamma \equiv \partial M/\partial \psi = \delta + \mu - g_{kx_1}(\partial x_1/\partial \psi)$$

$$= (\delta + \mu) + (g_{kx_1}/g_{x_1 x_1})$$

$$= [f'_1(k_1)k_2 - f_1(k_1) - f'_1(k_1)k_2]/(k_1 - k_2)$$

$$< 0 \quad \text{iff} \quad k_1 > k_2$$

In region C, $\dot{\psi} = 0$ implies

$$\psi(\delta + \mu) - g_k(0, k) \equiv M(\psi, k) = 0$$

The slope of the curve $\dot{\psi} = 0$ is given by

$$d\psi/dk = -(\partial M/\partial k)/(\partial M/\partial \psi) = g_{kk}/(\delta + \mu) < 0$$

In region I,

$$\dot{\psi} = \psi(\delta + \mu) - g_k - (g_{x_1} + \psi)f'_1 = \psi[\delta + \mu - f'_1(k)]$$

so that $\dot{\psi} = 0$ iff $k = k_B$ and $\dot{\psi} > 0$ if $k > k_B$, $\dot{\psi} < 0$ if $k < k_B$.

Now let us determine the shape and position of the curve $\dot{k} = 0$. In region C, $x_1 = 0$; hence $\dot{k} < 0$ for all $k > 0$. In region I, $x_1 = f_2(k)$; hence $\dot{k} = 0$ iff $k = \bar{k}$, where $\bar{k}$ is defined by

$$f_1(\bar{k}) = \mu k$$

In a region N, if $k > \bar{k}$, then $\dot{k} < 0$ because $x_1 = \rho f_1(k_1) < f_1(k)$. Thus in region N the curve $\dot{k} = 0$ is to the left of $k = \bar{k}$, and is the locus of points satisfying

$$x_1(\psi, k) - \mu k \equiv G(\psi, k) = 0$$

Its slope is

$$d\psi/dk = -(\partial G/\partial k)/(\partial G/\partial \psi)$$

where

$$\partial G/\partial k = -\mu + (\partial x_1/\partial k) = -\mu - (g_{x_1 k}/g_{x_1 x_1})$$

$$\partial G/\partial \psi = \partial x_1/\partial \psi = -1/g_{x_1 x_1} > 0$$

Thus

$$d\psi/dk = -[(x_1/k) + (g_{x_1k}/g_{x_1x_1})]g_{x_1x_1}$$
$$= [f_1(k_1)(k - \rho k_1) + \rho f_1(k_1)k_2]g_{x_1x_1}/(k_1 - k_2)$$
$$\gtreqless 0 \quad \text{iff} \quad k_2 \gtreqless k_1$$

The two curves $\dot{k} = 0$ and $\dot{\psi} = 0$ intersect at (k^*, ψ^*). The equilibrium has the regular saddlepoint property; see Fig. 2. It is possible that the stable branch of the saddlepoint intersects γ_I and γ_C many times, implying *multiple switching* into and out of the region of nonspecialization.

3.3 *Other Applications*

Apart from simple extension to the case of the world economy with or without factor mobility, but with a common rate of population growth, our function $g(x_1, k)$ may be used in models of exhaustible or renewable resources. For example, let R be the stock of an exhaustible resource, L = labor, M = the rate of extraction. Then

$$\dot{R} = -E, \quad \text{or,} \quad \dot{r} = -m - nr$$

where $r = R/L, m = M/L, n = \dot{L}/L$. Our function is

$$x_2 = g(x_1, m)$$

with all the properties listed in Section 2 (with k replaced by m). If the two goods x_1 and x_2 are traded at fixed world prices, then we obtain a generalization of Kemp and Long (1979) by allowing for population growth.

For another example, let the resource be renewable. Assume that $L = \bar{L}$ and

$$\dot{R} = X_1 + G(R) - M$$

where R is the resource stock, $G(R)$ the rate of natural growth, L is labor, M the rate of extraction, X_1 the renewal output and X_2 the output of the consumption goods. Then we can consider the problem

$$\max \int_0^\infty e^{-\delta t} g(x_1, m) \, dt$$

subject to

$$\dot{r} = x_1 - m + G(r)$$
$$x_1 \geq 0, \qquad f_1(m) - x_1 \geq 0$$

The solutions of the problem depend on the assumption about factor intensity. Again it is possible to have multiple switching into and out of the region of nonspecialization.

REFERENCES

Drandakis, E. M. (1963). Factor substitution in the two-sector growth model. *Review of Economic Studies* **30,** 217–228.

Hague, W. (1970). Sceptical notes on Uzawa's optimal growth in a two-sector model of capital accumulation. *Review of Economic Studies* **37,** 377–394.

Kemp, M. C., and Long, N. V. (1979). International trade with an exhaustible resource: A theorem of Rybczynski type. *International Economic Review* **20,** 671–677.

Long, N. V., and Vousden, N. (1977). Optimal control theorems. *In* "Applications of Control Theory to Economic Analysis" (J. D. Pitchford and S. J. Turnovsky, eds.), pp. 11–34. North-Holland Publ., Amsterdam.

Srinivasan, T. N. (1964). Optimal savings in a two-sector model of growth. *Econometrica* **32,** 358–373.

Uzawa, H. (1961). On a two-sector model of economic growth. *Review of Economic Studies* **29,** 40–47.

Uzawa, H. (1964). Optimal growth in a two-sector model of capital accumulation. *Review of Economic Studies* **31,** 1–24.

DEPARTMENT OF ECONOMICS
THE FACULTIES
AUSTRALIAN NATIONAL UNIVERSITY
CANBERRA, AUSTRALIA

Index

ECONOMIC THEORY, ECONOMETRICS, AND MATHEMATICAL ECONOMICS

Consulting Editor: Karl Shell

UNIVERSITY OF PENNSYLVANIA
PHILADELPHIA, PENNSYLVANIA